CREATING A PI COMMUNITY MEANS-ENDS CONNECTIONS TO FACILITATE THE ACQUISITION OF MORAL DISPOSITIONS

Developing, Living and Evaluating a Conceptual Framework in Teacher Education

Erskine S. Dottin

University Press of America,® Inc.
Lanham · Boulder · New York · Toronto · Oxford

TO

**CINDY and FARRELL
BERYL and GRAFTON**

CONTENTS

FOREWORD

Do you know the difference between a novice and an expert? The answers that readily come to mind might be that experts know more facts and have more experience working with those facts. These answers are partially true. According to the authors of an extensive study on "how people learn," the essence of the difference between an expert and a novice is that experts have a strong command of the facts in a given field *and* a conceptual understanding of those facts Brown and Cocking, 1990). It is the conceptual understanding that allows experts to more readily process and understand new information in a given area, to see patterns and relationships within and beyond their fields, and to think about their fields in critical and analytical ways. Conceptual understanding is a great tool for on-going learning and transference.

Consider the power of conceptual understanding in the context of the professional preparation of educators. If we prepare educators with not only the facts of their subject areas, but also with conceptual understanding of those subject areas and how to teach them, then we prepare educators who will become experts, who will be able to identify patterns and relationships within and between fields of study, who will be able to think about their fields in critical and analytical ways, and who will be flexible enough to understand and incorporate new information in the teaching and learning process. Think of the power of an educator equipped with subject area knowledge and this type of conceptual understanding in a classroom or school full of eager minds: Truly transformative.

If indeed schools, colleges, and departments of education (SCDEs) endeavor to prepare educators with this type of conceptual understanding, then SCDEs must approach the task from a conceptual perspective. To this end, the National Council for Accreditation of Teacher Education (NCATE) requires that accredited institutions develop and maintain a conceptual framework which provides a structure for all of the work in a given education unit.

The conceptual framework is designed to encourage institutions to articulate their goals; to ensure that the goals are professionally sound; to engage administrators, faculty, P-12 partners, and candidates in a coordinated effort to achieve the goals; and to evaluate candidate learning and program quality to determine whether the goals are being met. This conceptual approach to preparing educators, when actually lived in the life of the education unit, promotes alignment between what the unit is proposing to teach to candidates, the curriculum, the instruction, the field experiences, and the assessment. Theoretically, this alignment should foster deep learning and the preparation of experts; that is, the preparation of educators who can demonstrate mastery of content knowledge as well as a conceptual understanding of their fields and how to teach them.

Over the last 20 years, NCATE's understanding of this conceptual approach to teaching and learning has evolved. Currently, the conceptual framework is described as a living document having five structural elements. These elements include:

- Vision and mission of the institution and the unit;
- The unit philosophy, purposes, and goals;
- Knowledge bases, including theories, research, the wisdom of practice, and education policies;
- Candidate proficiencies aligned with the expectations in professional, state, and institutional standards;
- The system by which candidate performance is regularly assessed.

When NCATE examiners conduct accreditation visits, they assess the implementation of the conceptual framework, not as an individual standard, but rather as a component of all of the standards. Examiners conduct interviews with the educational community and review evidence such as assessments, assignments associated with field experiences, and faculty teaching methods. The examiners are working to determine whether the conceptual framework represents a shared vision; is providing coherence; is addressing professionally sound commitments and dispositions; and is a catalyst for adequately assessing proficiencies that are aligned with the standards of the specialized professional associations, with state standards, and with standards of the institution.

Individuals and institutions employ many different techniques in the development and maintenance of their conceptual frameworks. Some work by committee; some hold retreats with stakeholders; and some attend professional conferences. Some review examples of conceptual frameworks on the NCATE website. And some read books.

For individuals who are deeply interested in understanding the conceptual framework from a philosophical perspective steeped in Dewey and grounded in actual practice, this book will be invaluable. Erskine Dottin, known by many as the Father of the Conceptual Framework, has written a book that speaks to the moral imperative of designing and "living in" professional education units that are purposeful and coherent. Using the metaphor of a family living in a house, Dottin explores ways to link the structural elements of the conceptual framework to the NCATE standards. In so doing, he demonstrates the flexibility within the defined structure of the conceptual framework and the space for individuality within the delineated constructs of the NCATE standards. Through his ability to process and understand, to see patterns and relationships, to think critically and analytically about the conceptual framework, Dottin demonstrates his expertise in this most critical area of educator preparation.

Antoinette Mitchell, Associate Vice President, Accreditation Operations, National Council for Accreditation of Teacher Education (NCATE)

PREFACE

This book represents the continued conceptual journey of the author. I am grateful to John Dewey (1916/1944) for helping me realize that "Mind is not a name for something complete by itself; it is a name for a course of action in so far as that is intelligently directed – as aims, ends, enter into it, with selection of means to further the attainment of aims" (p. 132).

Along my journey, I have come to realize that "self-renewal" is more conducive to one's growth than is "reform," and that things may change but that does not guarantee growth. Consequently, I have come to the conclusion that "it is not what is poured into a pupil, but what is planted that counts."

I am also grateful to Peter Vaill (1996) *Learning as a way of being: Strategies for survival in a world of permanent white water* for bringing me back in my journey to the idea of systems thinking which suggests we cannot "describe a phenomenon independently of ourselves as perceivers without considering systemic interactions between ourselves and the phenomenon" that is part-whole relationships, and for reminding me that a conceptual framework should supply the kind of vision that will help to lift members of a community and bear them through turbulent and frustrating currents of white water.

ACKNOWLEDGMENTS

Insights for work such as this are not gained in isolation from others. In fact, it is the opportunity to listen to, read others' work, and engage in dialogue with others that forms the incubation and framework for one's own ideas and insights. I have grown in my conceptual journey from reading the work of persons such as Edward Clark, Stephen Covey, John Dewey, Robert DuFour, R.E. Fitzgibbons, Michael Fullan, John Goodlad, Laurie Beth Jones, Alfie Kohn, Jay McTighe, Louis Schmeir, Shari Tishman, Eileen Jay and D. N. Perkins, and Grant Wiggins; by listening to persons such as David Imig, Art Wise, and Hugh Sockett and by engaging in dialogue with the many participants and facilitators in the annual AACTE/NCATE Orientations, and the AACTE ad hoc committee Teacher Education as a Moral Community.

I am particularly moved by my colleagues at the following institutions and State Departments of Education who invited me to learn with and from them in their conceptual growth: Bloomsburg University, PA., California State University-Hayward, CA., California State University-Stanislaus, CA., Central Connecticut State University, CT., Claflin University, SC., Clayton College and State University, GA., The Citadel, SC., Frostburg State University, MD., Florida Memorial College, FL., Furman University, Kennesaw State University, GA., Kutztown University, PA., Georgia State University, GA., Grambling State University, LA., Howard University, Washington, DC., Millersville University, PA., North Carolina A&T University, NC., University of Northern Colorado, CO., Oakwood College, AL., The Ohio State University, OH., William Paterson University, Paterson University, NJ., Stetson University, FL., University of Miami, FL., University of Toledo, OH., Virginia State University, VA., Webster University, MO., University of Wyoming, WY., State Department of Education, Connecticut, Hawaii Teachers Standards Board, State Department of Education, South Carolina.

INTRODUCTION

Educational decisions concerning any aspect of preparation to meet the standards of the National Council for Accreditation of Teacher Education (NCATE) should be guided by an approach advocated by Robert Fitzgibbons which facilitates reasoning from certain outcomes that ought to occur in the teacher education program, to the conclusion that certain content ought to be taught, to the conclusion as to how that content should be taught, and how support units would best facilitate teaching that content in order to achieve those outcomes which ought to occur (Fitzgibbons, 1981).

Making educational decisions according to the foregoing approach assumes, therefore, that all of the very practical educational decisions that will be made in the educational unit will fall into one or another of the three categories of, outcomes or the aims of the endeavor, content or what is or could be taught and learned, and methods or the ways in which some content is or could be taught (Fitzgibbons, 1981).

Fitzgibbons cautions, however, that concerns about the outcomes, the matter and manner of education must focus on teaching and learning or in other words, the knowledge, skills, and dispositions to be taught and learned by candidates (Fitzgibbons, 1981), and thus candidate performance.

If one is asked to conceptualize about one's education unit and its programs then the foregoing structure shapes a paradigm that highlights the basic categories in education as seen below:

The WHY of the effort	Beliefs, Justification for beliefs, Ultimate aim, Educational outcomes
The WHAT of the effort	Knowledge (beliefs and understandings), Skills, Dispositions
The HOW of the effort	Effective methods (curricular and pedagogical knowledge)
The WHEN the why is achieved (what ought to minus what is)	Qualitative assessment indicators Quantitative assessment indicators

A focus on the NCATE accreditation review in the education of teachers and other school personnel reveals that the review process is about the quality of the unit in professional education as it pertains to the matter and manner of its candidates' performance, the faculty performance, the level and internal management of the unit's programs, fiscal, and physical resources and the unit's level of coherence.

By focusing on the unit, the NCATE review enhances the whole-part relationship between national accreditation and state program approval. The responsibility for reviewing the quality of the unit's preparation curricula and other program characteristics rests with the state approval agency. The whole-part relationship paradigm enables the existence of a program or an element that is not as strong as others to not automatically mean that the unit is without quality. The NCATE review of unit quality enables areas of improvement to be cited in the unit, and judgments be made regarding whether a sufficient number of areas of improvement should lead to provisional or conditional accreditation or accreditation denial for a unit. It is this whole-part relationship feature between national accreditation and state program approval that has eliminated a once serious criticism of redundancy in accreditation and state program approval. In fact, NCATE's agreements with 48 states, the District of Columbia, and Puerto Rico "are designed to mesh state and national professional expectations, and to eliminate duplication of effort on the part of the institution" (Frequently Asked Questions About NCATE, n.d.).

The whole-part relationship also enables the location of faculty and programs within the university not to be a relevant consideration in determining unit accreditation. It is essential however for the unit to demonstrate that all programs which prepare school personnel are controlled and coordinated by the teacher education unit, and that policies and requirements set by the teacher education unit are applied consistently across all programs. Faculty members and other instructional personnel assigned responsibilities in teacher education programs must meet qualifications set by the teacher education unit.

The education unit must, therefore, be in a position to conceptualize the what and the how of the curriculum, execute it through an educative process, and be responsible for the results.

This necessitates the unit being able to articulate a framework through which the interrelationships of the foregoing are made coherent and clear linkages and connections are demonstrated between and among the parts. In addition, this process should enable the unit to utilize the "state of the art" knowledge and accepted "best practices" that form a knowledge base for program operation, and to put in place an assessment and evaluation model that contributes to the utilization of assessment and evaluation results for program and unit change and growth.

One of the critical components of the NCATE standards, therefore, is a unit's ability to articulate and share a conceptual framework that provides direction for curriculum, programs, governance, etc. The idea of conceptual framework, while seen as very important in the teacher professional community, has presented difficulty for many institutions to translate and operationalize. Many institutions are in dire need of a work that would help guide not only their development of a conceptual framework, but their living according to their conceptual framework, and their being able to evaluate that conceptual framework.

Conceptual Framework

A conceptual framework may be construed as providing and bringing moral structure, coherence and consistency to experiences in a teacher education unit if it is seen as "a basic structure of ideas used to operationalize a teacher education program by systematically identifying and defining components and elaborating on the ways in which they are related" (Jewett & Mullan, 1977). A conceptual framework thus enhances continuous analysis of relationships among beliefs, between beliefs and actions, and relationships among actions. A conceptual framework is a way of thinking for oneself.

Every School/Department/College of Education, as a conceptual system, has a structure. Structure refers to a framework of related conceptual meanings and their generalizations that explain physical, natural, social and human realities. A conceptual framework, therefore, facilitates the fashioning of a coherent perspective into a unit by relating its parts into a coherent whole.

A conceptual framework is more than a **theme** (a subject or topic of discourse or of artistic representation) or a **model** (a set of plans for a building; a miniature representation of something). For example:

xvii

The model below provides a useful way of visualizing the many elements in a teacher preparation program; it helps order observations and data, and represents a generalized picture of complex interacting elements and sets of relationships.

The charge for teaching the curriculum	The content of the curriculum to be taught	The manner/methods in which the curriculum is taught
The evaluation of the curriculum	The persons to whom the curriculum is taught	The persons responsible for teaching the curriculum
The curriculum and its relationship to the world of practice	The administration of the curriculum	The evaluation of the unit responsible for the design and delivery of the curriculum

Instead, a conceptual framework establishes the purpose (the why) of a unit's efforts in preparing teacher education and school personnel candidates. The conceptual framework justifies why the elements are operationalized in a particular manner, and brings coherence to the elements in the model.

The literature shows that a key variable in effective programs is "coherence," that is, the extent to which curriculum, instruction, the integration of technology, and assessment and evaluation are aligned to form a coherent whole (Koppich & Knapp, 1998). Effective units and programs provide a conceptual framework (the common vision) that helps candidates to see the usefulness of their entire program, including the integration of field and clinical components and other elements of the professional preparation program.

A conceptual framework enables a unit to articulate and share with its professional community its way of seeing, thinking and being. This way of seeing, thinking and being encapsulates the sense of the unit across all unit programs. In addition, it sets forth the operational manner of the unit regarding what candidates should know (content knowledge) and be able to do (curricular, technological and pedagogical knowledge and skills), and the kinds of assessments and evaluation measures needed to produce the desired results in candidates' performance.

A unit's conceptual framework should, therefore, provide a sense of direction for the development and refinement of programs, courses, faculty teaching, research and service, candidates and faculty diversity, and unit accountability.

A conceptual framework enables a School/Department/College of Education to articulate the reasons for its existence: its underlying philosophy, its mission consistent with its institutional mission, its aim, learning outcomes for candidates in its programs that define what they should know and be able to do, and to what they should be disposed, the knowledge base(s) from sound research and best practice on teaching and learning upon which the learning outcomes are grounded, and the means by which the desired results in candidate performance will continuously be assessed and evaluated.

Structural Elements

If units view a conceptual framework as a way of seeing the world, that is, as a unit's frame of reference, then they will recognize the necessity of the unit having to articulate its desired future, its **vision**, and its underlying beliefs and values, its **philosophy**.

Since philosophy enables one to explore questions of existence, then the unit's conceptual framework should include the reason for its existence, its **aim**. Aims give rise to a unit examining why it is preparing its graduates. As a result, **learning outcomes** should be articulated, through **candidate learning proficiencies** that enable the unit to know what graduates should know (**understandings/knowledge**), be able to do (**skills**), and to what they should be disposed (**dispositions**). These learning outcomes should be grounded in a **knowledge base**. In other words, why the respective learning outcomes are important for a unit should be justified through the knowledge base for teacher education. In addition, these candidate proficiencies or **institutional standards** should manifest professional grounding by being aligned with state and professional standards promulgated by learned societies. Finally, the unit's way of thinking and living should make clear its **system of assessment and evaluation.**

The conceptual framework as a way of seeing, thinking and being thus enables units to move from questions of purpose (why) to questions of content (what) to questions of method (how).

In other words, in utilizing a conceptual framework, a unit states what is delivered in order to achieve its purpose. Consequently, a unit's assessment and evaluation system would entail its ascertaining whether its graduates were acquiring the learning outcomes, and as a result, would provide an understanding of whether the unit was achieving its overall aim, its purpose.

The unit might then be considered to be acting intelligently since "acting with an aim is all one with acting intelligently" (Dewey, 1916/1944, p. 103). In fact:

> A man is imperfectly intelligent when he contents himself with looser guesses about the outcome than is needful, just taking a chance with his luck, or when he forms plans apart from study of the actual conditions, including his own capacities. Such relative absence of mind means to make our feelings the measure of what is to happen. To be intelligent we must 'stop, look, listen' in making plans of an activity (Dewey, 1916/1944, p. 103).

Moral Coherence and Continuous Improvement

A teacher education unit's way of thinking about its purpose (why) and content (matter) and way of delivering the content (manner) should also engender ways of seeing and thinking about the culture of the unit in terms of candidate and faculty composition (diversity), faculty performance and development (scholarship of the classroom), the unit's will to govern, and the unit's capacity to provide necessary resources and facilities to achieve its aim.

A conceptual framework that enhances seeing and thinking in terms of the whole (the unit), to its parts (departments, programs, projects, committees, and so on), and back to the whole (the college/unit), also facilitates a unit's way of making meaning of its decision making in how it delivers its curriculum, how it attends to its candidates, how it enhances faculty vitality, and how unit accountability is provided.

In such a framework, goals planning for the unit is given meaning vis-à-vis what is delivered in order to achieve its aim. This goal focused model leads to a relationship between the unit, its departments and programs, and the products and goals each develops in order to enhance a unified and coherent operation.

The aim of a unit may thus be facilitated by a process of continuous improvement that moves from seeing the big unit picture, to the work of the unit to achieve its big picture goals through its parts (departments, programs, etc.), to the use of the results of the foregoing to effect change.

The use of a conceptual framework by a unit enriches its uniqueness. It also reinforces that while there may be many teacher education units, the ends agreed upon by the profession is the goal. The means to those ends may vary, and it is the use of a conceptual framework that provides units freedom to achieve and contribute to professional agreed upon ends in their own unique manner.

A conceptual framework therefore organizes thought processes in a unit. This way of seeing, thinking, and being should encapsulate the sense of the unit across all unit programs. It should provide a sense of direction for the development and refinement of programs, courses, faculty teaching, research, and service, candidates' performance, and unit accountability. In other words, a unit's conceptual framework should facilitate the fashioning of a coherent perspective into a unit by relating its parts into a coherent pattern or whole.

The conceptual framework as a unit's dominant meta-narrative or meta-schemata should not only contain explanations of and justifications for a unit's operations, that is ways of seeing and thinking about the world of professional education, but should also generate self-renewal possibilities for those involved (faculty, candidates, leadership).

In other words, a good conceptual framework will create possibilities for a unit to generate working hypotheses to guide the study of and subsequent renewal of its practices and policies. It is the compass for showing how the unit's operation will make life in the unit better for all involved.

CHAPTER ONE

THE MORAL QUESTION: HOW OUGHT LIFE TO BE LIVED IN YOUR UNIT?

"You can take a horse to the water but you cannot make it drink. You can take a person out of the penitentiary but you cannot make him/her penitent" (Dewey, 1944).

Moral Life in the Unit

The salient moral question in the development of a unit's conceptual framework is "how ought colleagues, candidates, staff, administrators, and relevant others live in the unit?" The response to this moral question brings to the fore the characteristics and dispositions seen as morally important in guiding life in the unit. In other words, the moral question helps the unit to consider the values it wants to encourage in its candidates through their thinking, behaving and feeling. More so, the moral question focuses attention on how candidates, faculty, and other personnel should behave ethically, and, therefore, on the highest good to which the unit aspires.

According to Lipman, Sharp and Oscanyan (1977):

> A moral life is [not] a journey by an individual with fixed identity towards certain fixed and unalterable goals. It is rather that the ends, which at any one time we hold to be desirable are held tentatively, and the self, at any one time, is always in a process of transition, contingent upon the means that are available to us to achieve the goals that are sought. Thus, the availability of means conditions and modifies our ideals and objectives, just as conversely, the ends we have in view control the way we search for means to employ, and the selves which we are in process of becoming (p. 15).

According to John Dewey, the moral suggests "... attention to what is done or intended, and ... to how or why the act is done" (Dewey, 1913, p. 5). The agent of a moral act:

> ... must know what he is doing... must choose it, and choose it for itself ... the act must be the expression of a formed and stable character. In other words, the act must be voluntary; that is, it must manifest a choice, and for full morality at least, the choice must be an expression of the general tenor and set of personality. It must involve awareness of what one is about; a fact which in the concrete signifies that there must be a purpose, an aim, and end in view, something for the sake of which the particular act is done (Dewey, 1960, p. 8).

In other words, "making moral judgments involves developing a sense of personal direction towards the goals that one foresees, however dimly, for oneself" (Lipman, Sharp, and Oscanyan, 1977, p. 15).

The answer to how one ought to live thus emerges as one makes a connection between means and ends. One must have some idea about the direction in which one wants to go or the desired future one sees.

The question about what ends should be pursued seems moot to many who just accept "what is":

> There are today multitudes of men and women who take their aims from what they observe to be going on around them. They accept the aims provided by religious teachers, by political authorities, by persons in the community who have prestige. Failure to adopt such a course would seem to many persons to be a kind of moral rebellion or anarchy. Many other persons find their ends practically forced upon them (Dewey, 1960, p. 29).

On the other hand, John Dewey notes that "There can, however, be no such thing as reflective morality except where men seriously ask by what purposes they should direct their conduct and why they should do so; what it is which makes their purposes good" (Dewey, 1960, pp. 29-30).

But to pursue an "end-in-view" should be separated from "mere anticipation or prediction of an outcome" and "the propulsive force of mere habit and appetite" (Dewey, 1960, p. 31):

Attainment of learning, professional skill, wealth, power, would not be animating purposes unless the thought of some result were unified with some intense need of the self, for it takes thought to convert an impulse into a desire centered in an object...on the other end, a strong craving tends to exclude thought... Deliberation and inquiry... take time; they demand delay, the deferring of immediate action. Craving does not look beyond the moment, but it is of the very nature of thought to look toward a remote end (Dewey, 1960, pp. 31-32).

The concept of "end" therefore "... implies something more or less distant, remote; it implies the need of looking ahead, of judging" (Dewey, 1960, p. 38). In other words:

... acting with an aim is all one with acting intelligently. To foresee a terminus of an act is to have a basis upon which to observe, to select, and to order objects and our own capacities. To do these things means to have a mind—for mind is precisely intentional purposeful activity controlled by perception of facts and their relationships to one another. To have a mind to do a thing is to foresee a future possibility; it is to have a plan for its accomplishment; it is to note the means which make the plan capable of execution and the obstructions in the way, or, if it is really a *mind* to do the thing and not a vague aspiration—it is to have a plan which takes account of resources and difficulties. Mind is capacity to refer present conditions to future results, and future consequences to present conditions. And these traits are just what are meant by having an aim or a purpose (Dewey, 1916/1944, p. 103).

So, how ought one live in the unit? Well, one way of answering the question is to visualize a social end in which "cultivation of power to join freely and fully in shared or common activities" (Dewey, 1916/1940, p. 123) is the ultimate end:

Any individual has missed his calling, farmer, physician, teacher, student, who does not find that the accomplishment of results of value to others is an accompaniment of a process of experience inherently worth while (Dewey, 1916/!944, p. 12).

In fact, Dewey points out that:

> ... every individual has grown up, and always must grow up, in a social medium. His responses grow intelligent, or gain meaning, simply because he lives and acts in a medium of accepted meanings and values. Through social intercourse, through sharing in the activities embodying beliefs, he gradually acquires a mind of his own. The conception of mind as a purely isolated possession of the self is at the very antipodes of the truth. The self *achieves* mind in the degree in which knowledge of things is incarnate in the life about him; the self is not a separate mind building up knowledge anew on its own account (Dewey, 1916/1944, p. 295).

In other words:

> When the social quality of individualized mental operations is denied, it becomes a problem to find connections which will unite an individual with his fellows. Moral individualism is set up by the conscious separation of different centers of life. It has its roots in the notion that the consciousness of each person is wholly private, a self-enclosed continent, intrinsically independent of the ideas, wishes, purposes of everybody else (Dewey, 1916/1944, p. 297).

If men and women ought to live in a manner that reinforces the idea that the rational and intellectual transcend the natural world of desires, feelings, activities, then the moral becomes linked to rational absolute principles and rules, or in other words, adhering to "authoritative guidance." The acquisition of knowledge, in the foregoing, is assumed to impact the acquisition of dispositions. The operational manifestation then is to have "the faculty of reason ... [be] endowed with power to influence conduct directly" (Dewey, 1916/1944, p. 298). And "since morality is concerned with conduct, any dualisms which are set up between mind and activity must reflect themselves in [a corresponding] theory of morals" (Dewey, 1916/1944, p. 346).

The proposal in this book is that we ought to live in a manner that enables us to acquire "habits that render our action [conduct] intelligent" (Dewey, 1916/1944, p. 344). We ought to live in a manner that enhances our growth through the application of our thinking to things already known for the purpose of improving social conditions. This requires the acquisition of *dispositions* both intellectual and social:

Only that which has been organized into our disposition so as to enable us to adapt the environment to our needs and to adapt our aims and desires to the situation in which we live is really knowledge. Knowledge is not just something which we are now conscious of, but consists of the dispositions we consciously use in understanding what now happens.

Knowledge as an act is bringing some of our dispositions to consciousness with a view to straightening out a perplexity, by conceiving the connection between ourselves and the world in which we live (Dewey, 1916/1944, p. 344).

Kardash and Sinatra (2003), for example, found in their studies that epistemological beliefs, that is, beliefs about knowledge, and cognitive dispositions, such as willingness to consider alternative points of view are positively correlated. In addition, Stanovich and colleagues, in their work, found that certain dispositional propensities are highly related to problem solving performance (Sa, West & Stanovich, 1999; Stanovich, 1999; Stanovich & West, 1997, 1998).

So as noted by Hugh Sockett, at his Pre-Conference Workshop sponsored by the Teacher Education as Moral Community Committee of the American Association of Colleges of Teacher Education, "the acquisition of dispositions is inherent in the process of education; it is not an add-on feature" (Sockett, 2004).

David Hansen (2001) captures the essence of the foregoing through his concept of "moral sensibility":

Conduct in teaching constitutes a pattern of action that supports meaningful teaching and learning. That pattern reflects, or emerges from, the teacher's agency, intentions, will, thought, feeling, imagination, and memory ... Person and conduct come to light in complementary fashion (p. 39).

In other words, according to Hansen (2001), "The moral quality of knowledge lies not in its 'possession,' ... but in how it can foster a widening consciousness and mindfulness" (p. 59). This "moral cast of mind," embodies commitments to "straightforwardness, simplicity, spontaneity, naiveté, open-minded, integrity of purpose, responsibility, and seriousness" (Hansen, 2001, pp. 45-56).

If "mindfulness" and "thoughtfulness" under-gird the work of teachers and other school personnel then units that prepare the foregoing personnel should be have the following goal as their top priority:

to assist their candidates to develop germane intellectual and social habits of mind that reinforce their being "mindful" and "thoughtful" teachers or other school personnel in "invitational environments" in the unit.

According to Barell (1991), the characteristics of thoughtful persons suggested by research on teaching and cognitive development are:

> They have confidence in problem-solving abilities.
> They persist.
> They control their own impulsivity.
> They are open to others' ideas.
> They cooperate with others in solving problems.
> They listen.
> They are empathic.
> They tolerate ambiguity and complexity.
> They approach problems from a variety of perspectives.
> They research problems thoroughly.
> They relate prior experience to current problems and make multiple connections.
> They are open to many different solutions and evidence that may contradict
>   favored points of view.
> They pose what-if questions, challenging assumptions and playing with variables.
> They are meta-cognitive: They plan, monitor, and evaluate their thinking.
> They are able to transfer concepts and skills from one situation to another.
> They are curious and wonder about the world. They ask 'good questions' (p. 34).

On the other hand, Max van Manen (1991) maintains that the qualities essential to pedagogical thoughtfulness are: "a sense of vocation, love of caring for children, a deep sense of responsibility, moral intuitiveness, self-critical openness, thoughtful maturity, tactful sensitivity toward the child's subjectivity, an interpretive intelligence, a pedagogical understanding of the child's needs, improvisational resoluteness in dealing with young people, a passion for knowing and learning the mysteries of the world, the moral fiber to stand up for something, a certain understanding of the world, active hope in the face of prevailing crises, and, not the least, humor and vitality" (p. 8).

The foregoing dispositions, therefore, reinforce the idea that:

> ... teaching is a moral endeavor that should be undertaken with skill. It does not comprise a set of value-neutral, discrete skills that should be carried out morally.... teaching is a practice that generates the need for particular skills and methods. It is not a set of occupational skills pieced together to fulfill a social function defined apart from those skills. The purposes of teaching both inform and come alive in method and technique (Hansen, 2001, p. 5).

Dispositions needed by teachers and other school personnel are the habits that will render their actions (conduct) intelligent in the world of practice, and as such, should guide how life is lived in a unit. How a unit's conceptual framework might be used to enhance these dispositions in the unit's professional community is the focus of the next chapter.

CHAPTER TWO

BUILDING MORAL COMMUNITY LIKE-MINDEDNESS

"We cannot give children a belief in themselves if the adults in the building feel powerless or victimized. The intellectual capacity of students can be no higher than the complexity of thought of the adults that surround them" (Author Unknown).

Means – Ends Link to Conceptual Framework

A conceptual framework enhances the making of moral judgments, and provides and brings moral structure, coherence and consistency to experiences in a unit if there is continuous analysis of relationships among beliefs, between beliefs and actions, and relationships among actions. In teacher education "many acts are done not only without thought of their moral quality but with practically no thought of any kind" (Dewey, 1960, p. 10).

So how ought colleagues, candidates, and relevant others conduct themselves in the unit? What should be the object of their desired end? Dewey notes, for example, that "The family in its moral aspects has one end, the common good of all its members" (Dewey, 1913, p. 571):

The family, for example, is something other than one person, plus another, plus another. It is an enduring form of association in which the members of the group stand from the beginning in relations to one another, and in which each member gets direction for his conduct by thinking of the whole group and his place in it, rather than by an adjustment of egoism and altruism.... Similar illustrations are found in business, professional, and political associations (Dewey, 1960, p. 164).

John Dewey offers an appropriate response for teacher educators vis-à-vis how they ought to conduct themselves in their respective units when he describes the concept of community (Dewey, 1916/1944):

Men live in a community in virtue of the things which they have in common; and community is the way in which they come to possess things in common. What they must have in common in order to form a community or society are aims, beliefs, aspirations, knowledge – a common understanding – like-mindedness as the sociologists say. Such things can not be passed physically from one to another, like bricks; they cannot be shared as persons would share a pie by dividing it into physical pieces. The communication which insures participation in a common understanding is one which secures similar emotional and intellectual dispositions – like ways of responding to expectations and requirements (Dewey, 1916/1944, p. 4).

Dewey goes on to say that:

Individuals do not even compose a social group because they all work for a common end. The parts of a machine work with a maximum of cooperativeness for a common result, but they do not form a community. If, however, they were all cognizant of the common end and all interested in it so that they regulated their specific activity in view of it, then they would form a community. But this would involve communication. Each would have to know what the other was about and would have to have some way of keeping the other informed as to his own purpose and progress (Dewey, 1916/1944, p. 5).

Dewey cautions, however:

Individuals use one another so as to get desired results, without reference to the emotional and intellectual disposition and consent of those used. Such uses express physical superiority, or superiority of position, skill, technical ability, and command of tools, mechanical or fiscal. So far as the relations of parent and child, teacher and pupil, employer and employee, governor and governed, remain upon this level, they form no true social group, no matter how closely their respective activities touch one another. Giving and taking orders modify action and results, but do not of itself effect a sharing of purposes, a communication of interests (Dewey, 1916/1944, p. 5).

Conceptualizing Unit Operations

The matter of how persons ought to conduct themselves in the unit brings to the fore once again the concept of whole-part relationships within a social context. If "the unit" is made analogous to Dewey's notion of "the family" then:

Interest in the social whole of which one is a member necessarily carries with it interest in one's own self. Every member of the group has his own place and work; it is absurd to suppose that this fact is significant in other persons but of little account in one's own case. To suppose that social interest is incompatible with concern for one's own health, learning, advancement, power of judgment, etc., is, literally nonsensical. Since each of us is a member of social groups and since the latter have no existence apart from the selves who compose them, there can be no effective social interests unless there is at the same time an intelligent regard for our own well-being and development (Dewey, 1960, p. 165).

If the unit is seen as a "family" or a system (a collective whole), then the individual parts emerge naturally (departments, programs – initial and advanced, etc.). Like the idea of "family," the unit becomes more than one faculty member, plus another faculty member, plus another. It becomes an "enduring form of association in which the members of the [unit] stand from the beginning in relations to one another, and in which each member gets direction for his [her] conduct by thinking of the whole ... and his [her] place in it, rather than by an adjustment of egoism and altruism (Dewey, 1960, p. 164).

According to Dewey:

> From the moral standpoint, the test of an industry is whether it serves the community as a whole, satisfying its needs effectively and fairly while also providing the means of livelihood and personal development to the individuals who carry it on. This goal could hardly be reached, however, if the business man (a) thought exclusively of furthering his own interest; (b) of acting in a benevolent way toward others; or (c) sought some compromise between the two....Services, in other words, would be reciprocal and cooperative in their effect (Dewey, 1960, p. 164).

The place of the individual faculty member or program in the moral life of the unit:

> ... is then, that the very problem of morals is to form an original body of impulsive tendencies into a voluntary self in which desires and affections center in the values which are common; in which interest focuses in objects that contribute to the enrichment of the lives of all (Dewey, 1960, p. 168).

The same idea vis-à-vis the individual and the common good is articulated by David Norton when he contends that "individual self-actualization is inherently social" (Norton, 1995, p. 134).

Furthermore, according to Norton, "The virtuous society [professional community] is a collective good that knits together, rather than circumventing, the goods of individuals" (p. 143).

So to conceptualize the unit as a moral community of departments, programs – initial and advanced, suggests that leadership by compulsion would have no moral standing in this context (Dewey, 1960). According to Dewey:

> Persons may and do yield to the demand of arbitrary force simply because they will suffer if they do not. But such yielding develops a slavish weakness in them and an arrogant disregard of the rights of others in those who have power (1960, 68).

Demands [external and internal] to which faculty members and programs in the unit will be subject need not proceed, therefore, from authoritative fiat:

> ...they may issue from the very nature of family life in the relation which exists between parent and offspring. Then they do not come to the child as an external and despotic power, but as expressions of a whole to which he himself belongs. He is moved to respond by his affection for his parents, by his respect for their judgment; even when the demand runs contrary to his uppermost desire he still responds to it as to something not wholly alien. Because of inherent relationships persons sustain to one another, they are exposed to the expectations of others and to the demands in which these expectations are made manifest (Dewey, 1960, p. 69).

Dewey's notion of the family as community points to the moral aspect of having an aim, and the acquisition of meaning within a social context. For example, Dewey (1916/1944) notes that if one person just threw a ball to another without any aim in view then such behavior is not "meaningful." On the other hand, if the individuals have as their social aim the development of a baseball team to compete in a league tournament then the activity of ball throwing becomes meaningful in light of the social aim. A means to that aim include the acquisition of knowledge about baseball, requisite skills, and dispositions of sportsmanship.

So the means-ends connections vis-à-vis the development of a conceptual framework in the unit may be captured accordingly:

Means-Ends Connections

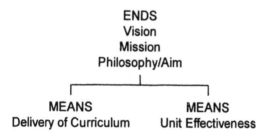

ENDS
Vision
Mission
Philosophy/Aim

MEANS   MEANS
Delivery of Curriculum   Unit Effectiveness

These means-ends connections may be delineated in even further detail so that links may be made to the standards promulgated by the National Council for Accreditation of Teacher Education (NCATE, 2002).

MEANS –ENDS CONNECTIONS
ENDS
Mission
Vision
Philosophy/Aim

MEANS   **MEANS**
Delivery of Curriculum   Unit Effectiveness
Outcomes   Goals
Knowledge base(s)
Candidate proficiencies and
Alignment with state and
Professional standards
System of assessment

The foregoing means-ends connections may therefore be attached to the description in the NCATE Standards (2002) which outlines the structural elements of a conceptual framework.

These standards indicate that a conceptual framework should provide the following structural elements:

- the vision and mission of the institution and unit;
- the unit's philosophy, purposes, and goals;
- knowledge bases, including theories, research, and the wisdom of practice, and education policies;
- candidate proficiencies aligned with the expectations in professional, state, and institutional standards;
- the system by which candidate performance is regularly assessed (NCATE, 2002, p. 12).

The elements delineated above in bullets one and two point to desirable ends. The elements in bullets three, four and five point to the means by which the ends may be achieved.

The means-ends connection in the structural elements of the conceptual framework must be grounded in the understanding that the connection is continuous. In other words, the end is not to be seen as an externally imposed end which might lead to a separation between ends and means. Instead, the means-end connection shown here is to be construed as Dewey (1916/1944) suggests:

> ... an end which grows up within an activity as plan for its direction is always both ends and means, the distinction being only one of convenience. Every means is a temporary end until we have attained it. Every end becomes a means of carrying activity further as soon as it is achieved. We call it end when it marks off the future direction of the activity in which we are engaged; means when it marks off the present direction. Every divorce of end from means diminishes by that much the significance of the activity and tends to reduce it to drudgery from which one would escape if he could (p. 106).

The Desired Future

Kerka (2003) a key leader in the area of "Appreciative Inquiry," contends that appreciative inquiry engages people and organizations in discovering what gives life to human systems when they are most effective and constructive and using that knowledge to envision and create the preferred future. According to Kerka (2003), appreciative inquiry assumes that reality is socially constructed. Consequently, it may be inferred that organizations evolve in the direction of the images people in the organization create. In other words, in this context, behavior in the present is influenced by the anticipated future.

Block (1987) maintains that "creating a vision forces us to take a stand for a preferred future" (p. 102). As a result, the unit's desired future for its initial and advanced programs, that is, its vision/theme should emerge as a result of collaborative dialogue among the faculty and members of its professional community. This collaborative endeavor should be framed by Peter Senge's exhortation that learning organizations are synonymous with shared visions (Senge, 1990). In fact, Michael Fullan contends: "Shared vision is important in the long run, but for it to be effective you have to have something to share. It is not a good idea to borrow someone else's vision" (Fullan, 1993, p. 13).

The first element, therefore, of a unit's conceptual framework is a description of what the unit wants to become. According to Peterson (1995) this description of a unit's desired future is captured in a vision statement.

However, a vision is not a strategic plan. A strategic plan contains goals and objectives which tell how and when some goal will be achieved. A vision, therefore, is a shared sense of the future. It reflects the qualities that make the community unique; the kind of conditions and results the community hopes will exist in the future.

Kerka suggests that one way to articulate a vision is to envision what life in the unit might be like if the unit were functioning at its best, healthiest [peak moments], and then use that knowledge to create a preferred future (Kerka, 2003). An example of this process may be seen in the vision articulated by The Lion and the Lamb Peace Arts Center of Bluffton College, Bluffton, Ohio: "I dream of a peaceable kingdom in which people give birth to children who ask, 'Mother, what was war'?" ("I Dream," n.d.).

It is important to note that the key components of a well articulated vision statement are the targeted population, the desired conditions and the anticipated results in the desired future. Consequently, the foregoing vision statement reveals human beings as the targeted population, peace as the desired conditions, and no more war as the anticipated results.

On the other hand, the statement below presented by a unit as a vision statement does not convey the same components of targeted population, desired conditions and anticipated results:

The College of Education consists of a world-class team of educators who provide innovative research, teaching, service, and leadership to the local community, the State, the Nation, and the world beyond. The College prepares educators to contribute to the advancement of a diverse humanity in realizing a just and democratic society.

The above statement seems more focused on the composition of members of the unit and the services they provide. The second sentence in the statement offers a limited clue to the envisioned targeted population, and anticipated results. In other words, the desired future envisioned at The Lion and the Lamb Peace Arts Center seems clearer in answering the question "how ought we live?" than does the statement offered by the anonymous unit.

The desired future contained in the vision of North Glade Elementary School, in Miami-Dade County Public Schools is even clearer:

North Glade Elementary School will be a harbor for learners – teachers, students and parents who explore the world around them in harmonious, interconnected learning communities, questioning and seeking answers, and continuously working toward a common goal of bringing passion and joy into every classroom by seeing the world of possibility within each learner. It is envisioned that North Glade Elementary will be a nurturing, safe place that assists children to reach the potential they never knew they had; a place   where teachers are motivated to teach and students are motivated to learn; where teachers encourage independence, passion, and pride; where excellence is sought and failure is merely a step to understanding; where every member brings valued resources to the school and is recognized by all other members; and where academic performance is just as important as the skills gained through life experiences (North Glade Elementary, n.d.).

Peter Senge, in his book, *The Fifth Discipline*, suggests that the salient question in pursuing a vision is the question, "why" (1990). In fact, he argues that purpose and vision cannot be separated because a why without a desired future lacks a sense of appropriate scale, and a desired future without a why lacks passion (Senge, 1990).

Vision Building

There are many activities that are conducive to helping a unit design and develop a vision. One of those activities, as outlined by DuFour and Eaker (1998) may be conducted accordingly. Have each member of the unit write a descriptor of what he/she hopes the unit will become. The descriptor may address initial and advanced preparation levels together or separately. Unit participants may be assisted in this process by asking them to think of the following questions: What would you like to see the unit become? What reputation would it have? What contribution would it make to candidates and its community? What values would it embody? How would people work together?

DuFour and Eaker (1998) further suggest that the unit then be divided into small groups so that the groups might do the following. Each of these small groups should discuss the desired future descriptors of each group member and capture a statement that best describes the group's collective vision. A committee then collects all of the group statements, and develops a draft of a vision statement based on a common theme in the small group statements. This committee's draft is then shared with the entire faculty, and members of the unit's community for critique, and suggested revisions.

The unit committee then revises its draft vision statement based on the foregoing suggestions and offers a second draft for comment. If the majority accepts the draft then the unit may use the vision statement as the design and guide for its operation - the preparation of professional educators. A version of this activity was carried out by professional education unit faculty at California State University - Stanislaus, in the spring of 2000, in that unit's quest for a revised vision/theme and outcomes.

An additional activity for a unit in its design and development of a vision statement is to have each department, related school/college, endorse the common vision statement. In turn, each department and program in the unit can then use the process to develop its own statement for the department and program(s) vis-à-vis what they want to become. Each designed and developed department and program(s) statement must then show its consistency with the unit's vision.

VanGundy (1998), on the other hand, proposes a method of brainstorming as a vehicle for building a vision. This method may be seen as an extension of DuFour and Eaker's (1998).

On the other hand, Zmuda, Kuklis, and Kline (2004) suggest the "putting together of a focus group ... to move all participants from their individual roles as stakeholders (individual autonomy) to a common role of shared responsibility (collective autonomy" (p. 61). To these authors, the focus group process in vision building:

> ... is a mode of operation in which people generally collaborate in pursuit of shared goals and interests that serve the individual and the system. The school as a system becomes a united body in its determination to achieve the desired results but still fosters open inquiry and individual creativity. Collective autonomy is a hallmark of a competent system. A competent system proves itself when everyone within the system performs better as a result of the collective endeavors and accepts accountability for that improvement (Zmuda, Kuklis & Kline, 2004, pp. 61-62).

"Collective autonomy" as the catalyst in the pursuit of a desired future might be operationalized through the following activity for members of a unit.

> In small groups, members of a unit would explore the following:
> 1. In your dream of the unit, how ought you live? What desired conditions do you hope for?
> 2. What do you see as the targeted population with whom the unit should work?
> 3. What kind of results do you see for the unit? What contribution would it make to candidates and its community?
> The responses of all groups would be synthesized to produce a comprehensive statement that captures the essence of unit members' responses to the question.

The outcome of any of the foregoing vision building activities is a unit that is instilled with a sense of direction and destination, that has a target of purpose, and in which there is widespread ownership of that direction. Nanus (1992) cautions, however, that while:

> Vision plays an important role ... throughout the organization's entire life cycle....

Sooner or later the time will come when an organization needs redirection or perhaps a complete transformation, and then the first step should always be a new vision, a wake-up call to everyone involved with the organization that fundamental change is needed and is on the way (p. 9).

Allen (2001) reminds us that: "Almost everyone in the education community agrees that people associated with schools would benefit from having a common vision to guide their individual and collective actions" (p. 290). The same author contends that: "It seems that everyone agrees that school communities should have some sort of covenant, vision, mission, philosophy, or values to guide their work" (Allen, 2001, p. 290). However, Allen (2001) notes that most visions gather dust because they are not used to breathe life in a community's conduct, actions, and daily behaviors:

A school's work with student assessment, staff development, teacher evaluation, hiring, mentoring programs, communicating with parents, and so forth is most powerful when efforts in all these areas are aligned with its guiding statements. What message does it send to teachers when they are evaluated according to something other than a school's guiding statements? Or when staff development activities are inconsistent with the school's guiding statements? How are parents supposed to be meaningful partners in their children's education when they aren't given opportunities to help bring a school's statements to life? How can students take their school's guiding statements seriously when their teachers' assessment instruments aren't aligned with the guiding statements? (p. 292).

Capturing Vision in a Theme

A unit's desired future may be captured in a theme. A theme may be construed of as an effective means to communicate the essence of a vision, and an easy way for people to remember the vision. For example, let us revisit the vision for North Glade Elementary:

North Glade Elementary School will be a harbor for learners – teachers, students and parents who explore the world around them in harmonious, interconnected learning communities, questioning and seeking answers, and continuously working toward a common goal of bringing passion and joy into every classroom by seeing the world of possibility within each learner.

It is envisioned that North Glade Elementary will be a nurturing, safe place that assists children to reach the potential they never knew they had; a place where teachers are motivated to teach and students are motivated to learn; where teachers encourage independence, passion, and pride; where excellence is sought and failure is merely a step to understanding; where every member brings valued resources to the school and is recognized by all other members; and where academic performance is just as important as the skills gained through life experiences (North Glade Elementary, n.d.).

How might the essence of the foregoing be communicated in an easy way so that people may remember the vision? The personnel at North Glade Elementary decided that the essence of their vision statement might be communicated in a simple manner through the following theme: *From School House to School Home.*

The vision of life lived in a school house is obviously quite different from that lived in a school home. The essence of such life in a school home is thus captured in the comprehensive vision statement.

If the concept of conceptual framework is interpreted to be a unit's dominant meta-narrative or meta-schemata that not only contains explanations of and justifications for a unit's operations, that is ways of seeing and thinking about the world of professional education, but also generates self-renewal possibilities for those involved (faculty, candidates, leadership) then it is critical to understand that a theme, a metaphorical representation of a comprehensive vision statement, is not the conceptual framework.

So where is your unit in terms of the path toward its vision? Laurie Beth Jones (1996) warns that "People who focus mostly on 'what is' will create more of 'what is.' People who focus mostly on 'what could be' will begin to create 'what could be' (p. 94).

Is your unit keeping its eyes on its prize, its desired future? Where would you place your unit, presently, along the following continuum?

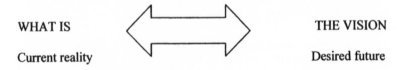

WHAT IS   THE VISION

Current reality   Desired future

Articulating the Unit Mission

While the unit's vision or theme communicates a desired future, the unit's mission statement, describes what the unit is charged to do.

A vision or theme is, therefore, not a mission. A mission statement is basically a broad general statement of purpose which specifies a unit's reason(s) for existence and establishes the scope of a unit's activities. A unit's mission statement should in some way be congruent with the mission statement of the institution in which the unit resides. DuFour and Eaker (1998) maintain that:

> The mission question challenges members of a group to reflect on the fundamental purpose of the organization, the very reason for its existence. The question asks, 'Why do we exist?' "What are we here to do together?' and 'What is the business of our business?' The focus is not on how the group can do what it is currently doing better or faster, but rather on why it is doing it in the first place. Addressing this question is the first step in clarifying priorities and giving direction to everyone in the organization (58).

While the unit's vision of teaching and learning provides a sense of the unit's desired future, its mission delineates the specific task with which it is charged and offers its raison d'etre, its sense of purpose. In its development of a mission, a unit can direct its activity to two areas (a) tradition within the academy, and (b) state directives for colleges of education.

Tradition in universities, of which colleges of education are a part, calls for a strong commitment to excellence in teaching, research, and service. A unit's translation of its interpretation of its commitment to excellence in teaching, research, and service should therefore be delineated in its purpose, its mission. A unit may, therefore, examine its university's traditional commitment to excellence in teaching, research, and service and develop its own special meaning, identity and sense of itself as a professional community vis-à-vis its commitment to excellence in teaching, research, and service. The need to enhance scholarship is a part of a unit's mission.

On the other hand, historical state directives have charged colleges of education to educate and prepare teachers, administrators, and other school personnel to function as competent, creative, and knowledgeable facilitators of learning, leadership, etc. A unit may also look to its state directive for direction in its development of a mission statement.

Mission statements should clearly delineate the unit's purpose for its existence in terms of (a) who is to be served – the customers, (b) the services to be provided, and (c) how the services are to be provided – the activities. Can you clearly detect the foregoing elements in the mission statement below?:

> North Glade Elementary like all other public schools exists to serve public goals, that is, the collective good of a democratic society. These goals are determined by elected representatives in local, state, and federal governments. More specifically, the mission at North Glade Elementary, given current public goals, is to continually improve student academic performance to ensure that all students demonstrate mastery of grade level material, making a minimum of one year's academic growth annually (North Glade Elementary, n.d.).

Can you detect the components in this mission statement?:

> The College of Education promotes human development within the context of a multicultural, democratic society. The mission of the College is to: Prepare and provide ongoing professional development of teachers, administrators, counselors and related professionals at the undergraduate and graduate levels; Generate, synthesize and apply knowledge in education and related fields through teaching, research and other scholarly activities, and Provide service and support to the local, national and global educational and related communities.

How would you improve the language in each mission statement to better articulate the components of customers to be served, services to be provided, and the means for those services? Does the following statement improve things?

> The College of Education, like all other public colleges, exists to serve the public good in the State of XX. More specifically, the mission of the College of Education at XX, given current state goals, is to prepare teachers and other school personnel (at the initial and advanced levels) who are exemplary models of educational best practices in classrooms and other educational venues throughout the state, nation, and the globe.
> The College of Education is thus charged by both state and institutional directives to produce educators for democratic institutions who are able to generate, synthesize, and apply knowledge in education and related fields. Faculty in the unit are thus charged to enhance this mission through teaching, research and other creative activities, and service and support to local, national and global educational related communities.

Is the mission statement for your unit clearly stated? Is it easy in your unit's mission statement to detect the reason for its existence, and the charge regarding the customers to be served, the services to be offered, and the means through which the services are provided? Is your unit's mission compatible with the mission of your institution?

Mission Building Process

Members of a unit might follow these steps in developing a mission statement for a unit. First, unit members in small groups might explore state and university directives with which the unit is charged vis-à-vis: who is to be served (customers), what services are to be provided (services), and how are the services to be provided (activities)? A university's or college's charge vis-à-vis teaching, research and service should also be considered with regard to customers, services and activities.

A synthesis of all responses to the foregoing should be outlined in a short statement that explains why the unit exists, that gives special meaning, identity, and sense of self while being consistent with State directives and University commitments.

Building the Unit Philosophy

John Dewey maintains that while science influences conduct through laws of science, facts, things to do or not do; philosophy means achieving a wisdom which would influence the conduct of life in the unit [moral/ethical dimensions] (Dewey, 1916/1944, pp. 324-325).

Is there a center from which the unit approaches the life of the teacher and other school personnel preparation? In other words, are there underlying commitments to any set of philosophical, psychological and pedagogical beliefs? Does the unit offer reasons through these commitments for its approach to the life of the teacher and other school personnel preparation?

The next structural element of a conceptual framework is, therefore, the *why* of the unit's efforts - its philosophy. The unit's philosophy should enable one to get a sense of the general underlying beliefs in the unit about reality, truth and knowledge, ethics and values which give meaning to the unit's existence, and which form the bases for critical decisions.

A philosophy of education vis-à-vis the unit's philosophy is a set of beliefs about reality, truth and knowledge and ethics and value; about how human beings come to know and learn; and about best pedagogical practices.

This element of the conceptual framework may therefore be construed as the justification for the lens through which the unit sees the world of teaching and learning.

If the unit's vision/theme is thought of as the first creation in the development of a conceptual framework, then the values and principles upon which the unit's being and doing will be based may be seen as the second creation, that is, the road map to coherent construction of the framework. Here the unit begins to delineate the basis for its decisions, and consequently begins to give meaning to its professional world through philosophical lens. As a result, the unit's philosophical lens provides an underlying aim for its conceptualization of teaching and learning, knowledge and truth, and learning outcomes vis-à-vis institutional standards.

John Dewey noted that philosophy implies "a certain totality, generality, and ultimateness," and "is the endeavor to attain as unified, consistent, and complete an outlook upon experience as is possible" (Dewey, 1944, 324). Dewey further noted:

> This direct and intimate connection of philosophy with an outlook upon life obviously differentiates philosophy from science. Particular facts and laws of science evidently influence conduct. They suggest things to do and not to do, and provide means of execution. When science denotes not simply a report of the particular facts discovered about the world but a *general attitude* toward it - as distinct from special things to do - it merges into philosophy. For an underlying disposition represents an attitude not to this and that thing nor even to the aggregate of known things, but to the considerations which govern conduct (Dewey, 1944, 324-325).

If Dewey is correct, then units are delineating their general outlook upon life in teacher education in which there is a large faculty commitment to the underlying tenets of that outlook and through which the unit evinces "certain distinctive modes of [professional] conduct" (Dewey, 1944, 324). This normative outlook challenges members in a unit to escape the immediacy of "how" and move to underlying values and principles vis-à-vis "the why."

So how ought life be lived in the unit? How might members of the unit's community give life to their educational aims in practice? Ivie (2003) contends that "Our daily activities – thinking, acting, teaching and learning – are supersaturated with metaphors" (p. 1). His work brings clearly to focus that the language of education abounds with metaphors. For example, suppose an educator believes a teacher is like a gas pump attendant, then it seems that learning will be measured on the basis of what is pumped into the student. On the other hand, if an educator believes a teacher is a tour guide then measuring learning on the basis of what is pumped in would seem quite odd. In the first metaphor, the process of learning might be better identified with a transfer theory of learning, while the second metaphor induces an experiential theory of learning. Ivie (2003) warns that business leaders have demanded that schools become more accountable. However, he notes that such a demand can best be accomplished only by adopting a metaphor and "the philosophy of the marketplace" (p. 5).

Means to Articulating a Philosophy

Educational decisions regarding purpose (why), content (what), and method (how), are related to the beliefs of the person who makes such decisions. A philosophy of education might, therefore, be seen as a set of beliefs of educational purpose, content, and method. Consequently, it is from the unit's philosophy of education, its beliefs about education, that it offers rational educational decisions. A unit's philosophy of education must, therefore, contain two distinct kinds of beliefs: (1) philosophical beliefs regarding reality (metaphysics), truth and knowledge (epistemology), and values (axiology), and (2) empirical beliefs (psychological, sociological, and pedagogical).

By articulating a philosophy of education the unit is offering intelligent justification for choosing and making particular educational decisions. In other words, the unit's philosophy brings to the fore that thinking is not separated from doing something with a purpose in mind. When a unit possesses an educational philosophy, and is able to identify the underlying metaphysical, epistemological and axiological assumptions upon which that philosophy is built, that unit is able to bring a certainty to its behavior because its behavior is congruent with its philosophy.

That behavior, whether it is in the areas of curriculum, candidate activities, personnel matters, and so on, becomes a natural outcome of the unit's philosophy, and is, therefore, an extension, reflection, and reinforcement of that philosophy, that is, the unit's wisdom in practice. So does the vision/theme and mission suggest underlying commitments to any particular philosophical, psychological, or pedagogical beliefs? Are there any general underlying beliefs about reality, truth and knowledge, ethics and values that give meaning to the unit's existence and/or that form the bases for critical decisions, that is, the center from which the unit approaches the life of teacher and other school personnel preparation?

For example, let us revisit the desired future contained in the vision statement at North Glade Elementary:

> North Glade Elementary School will be a harbor for learners – teachers, students and parents who explore the world around them in harmonious, interconnected learning communities, questioning and seeking answers, and continuously working toward a common goal of bringing passion and joy into every classroom by seeing the world of possibility within each learner. It is envisioned that North Glade Elementary will be a nurturing, safe place that assists children to reach the potential they never knew they had; a place where teachers are motivated to teach and students are motivated to learn; where teachers encourage independence, passion, and pride; where excellence is sought and failure is merely a step to understanding; where every member brings valued resources to the school and is recognized by all other members; and where academic performance is just as important as the skills gained through life experiences (North Glade Elementary, n.d.).

North Glade Elementary used the following framework (developed by Erskine Dottin) as a tool to lay out its philosophy.

Elements of Philosophy	
Use of a metaphor to conceptualize teaching and learning	
How learning will be facilitated	Justification/support [psychological, philosophical, pedagogical]
The kind of person the unit is trying to produce	Justification/support [psychological, philosophical, pedagogical]
Translating beliefs into pedagogical action	Justification/support [psychological, philosophical, pedagogical]
The underlying aim	

Recall that the personnel at North Glade Elementary decided that the essence of their vision statement might be communicated in a simple manner through the following theme: *From School House to School Home.*

So is there an underlying metaphor that emerges from the vision and theme at North Glade Elementary? In an attempt to give life to their educational thought and beliefs through practice,   faculty and administrators at the school all articulated the metaphor each person thought best captured his/her response to the statement "Teaching and learning as ... " or "Teaching and learning is like ...." The community then looked for the metaphor and explanation that seemed most common, and that was related to the community's vision and theme. As a result, the community identified its metaphor as "Teaching and learning at North Glade Elementary is like leading a family life." To the community this meant:

> A good family sets goals for its members, and it works towards a common goal. Each member brings strengths to the family, and correspondingly finds strength in other family members. Like a patchwork quilt, so too does a family contain members who come in a variety of shapes, colors, textures, and patterns. Teachers must accept that no two children are alike. Every child does not learn in the same manner. Just as families stick together, exhibit good teamwork, and express feelings and emotions to and with each other, so too in teaching and learning there should be lots of caring, understanding, and attention. The fabrics of the teaching and learning environment are like fabrics of a quilt, interconnected to form a whole – a family. Just as parents should be role models for their children, so too must teachers be for students; they must nurture the self-esteem of all learners. They must engender a "sky is the limit" perspective in each child, while concurrently serving a well-balanced educational diet. Like good parents do with their children, teachers must guide learners to do things on their own – be independent, and thus realize their full potential through different routes (Unpublished document, n.d.).

To extend its philosophy, the North Glade Elementary community extended its metaphor by providing justification for empirical beliefs drawn from relevant and related schools of psychology and pedagogy, and for philosophical beliefs drawn from relevant and related schools of philosophy.

This justification is framed by the articulation of (a) beliefs about how learning occurs (b) how learning will be facilitated to achieve the unit's outcomes, and (c) the pedagogical activities that will best enhance the unit achieving its psychological and philosophical ends. Inherent in this philosophical justification, therefore, is the North Glade Elementary community's answer to the moral question, "how ought people at North Glade Elementary to conduct themselves." Below are excerpts from the North Glade Elementary philosophy.

Beliefs: How learning occurs (at North Glade, Elementary)

Teachers and other school personnel at North Glade Elementary seen as members of a family in a good home motivate by transmitting required knowledge needed for students to master their grade level content. They facilitate a learning process that leads to their restructuring how students think about their content through multi-sensory learning experiences and approaches. Since they care deeply about the mature growth of the immature members of the family, they act as friends and nurturers to help these immature members develop necessary basic learning skills and dispositions. They proffer an invitational style to classrooms and the school.

To see teaching and learning as motivating is to believe that human beings are naturally motivated, and the role of the teacher is to simply capture and utilize the motivation that is already there. More specifically, it is assumed that all human beings are not at the same point in their development, and consequently, require different motivational means (Ozmon & Craver, 1990). Motivating the young to know and understand does not mean having them ingest subject matter in which they have little interest. Such procedures tend to induce what John Dewey terms "Motivation through rewards extraneous to the thing to be done...." (Dewey, 1916/1944, p. 177). There is considerable evidence to suggest that such external inducements have little effect on internal interests. To motivate from the metaphorical perspective of teaching and learning as leading a family life suggests "The desirability of starting from and with the experience and capacities of learners...." (Dewey, 1944, p. 194). In fact, Dewey maintains that teaching and learning is interaction between the teacher's knowledge of the subject and their pupils' needs and capacities:

Processes of instruction are unified in the degree in which they center in the production of good habits of thinking. While we may speak without error, of the method of thought, the important thing is that thinking is the method of an educative experience.

The essentials of method are therefore identical with the essentials of reflection. They are first that the pupil have a genuine situation of experience – that there be a continuous activity in which he is interested for its own sake; secondly, that a genuine problem develop within this situation as a stimulus to thought; third, that he possess the information and make the observations needed to deal with it; fourth, that suggested solutions occur to him which he shall be responsible for developing in an orderly way; fifth, that he have the opportunity and occasion to test his ideas by application, to make their meaning clear and to discover for himself their validity (Dewey, 1944, p. 163).

Teaching as motivating, facilitating and nurturing family goals and needs induces learning as a kind of pedagogy where the emphasis is more on what students do than on what teachers do, and where there is assessment of student learning rather than an over emphasis on standardized achievement testing (Iran-Nejad, 1995). In this context, the predominant teaching model is not one in which teachers simply transfer knowledge to students, a form of pupil 'reception and compliance.' In the 'reception and compliance' model of learning, according to Iran-Nejad (1995): 'the teacher's performance in front of students is critical, and in many school districts teachers are evaluated for their ability to establish effective eye contact, use different kinds of questions, pause in explanations to allow pupil reflection, use a variety of concepts, and redirect student questions, and so forth – a process of disassembling knowledge into small bits for students to comprehend' (p. 18).

The model of teaching and learning, envisioned at North Glade Elementary brings to the foreground the students instead of the teachers. Teaching as motivating, facilitating and nurturing helps students to explore, organize and monitor their own learning (Iran-Nejad, 1995). It also helps teachers to focus more on students' understanding, as they facilitate students' thinking and problem solving (Iran-Nejad, 1995).

Teaching as motivating, facilitating, and nurturing at North Glade Elementary is, ..., supported by Piaget's concept of assimilation and accommodation, that is, attention to students' developmental readiness and their cognitive development (Piaget & Inhelder, 1970; Piaget, 1959); and by Gardner's notion of multiple intelligences (Gardner, 1985). In this context, students learn through a discovery thematic/project approach: for example, if they are studying trees, they will go outside and take a look at trees rather than simply observe pictures in a book – the school campus and community become a learning laboratory. Learning in this context presupposes family and intergenerational involvement; cooperative learning endeavors; and multiage learning activities.

Intentions: How Learning is Facilitated (North Glade Elementary)

Teaching as motivating, facilitating, and nurturing at North Glade Elementary is thus compatible with the philosophical notions of Carl Rogers – learning through exploration and progressing at one's own level (Rogers, 1982), and with the philosophical ideas of John Dewey – scientific learning and thinking by doing (Dewey, 1944).

Teachers and staff at North Glade, therefore, have as their primary goal to encourage students' creative and critical thinking. They teach with expectations of some product of student learning in view. They act as facilitators responsible for assessing and evaluating learning and communicating to students what is to be learned. They seek to achieve goals collaboratively with students, and they create learning environments that are demonstrative of sensitivity to and respect for all learners.

Teaching and learning at North Glade pursues educational ends in which students become successful, confident, inquisitive, organized, prepared, creative, motivated, respectful, responsible, and caring individuals.

Actions: How to go about doing what is to be accomplished (North Glade Elementary)

Philosophical and psychological ends at North Glade are therefore manifested in, and through, the following pedagogical means: flexible grouping of furniture and kids and changing room designs; inviting classrooms; learning centers; hands-on, experiential activities; problem-solving and decision-making activities that incorporate technology; cross-curriculum/interdisciplinary learning; cooperative learning; class projects; activity-oriented and product-based pursuits; teachers modeling expected behaviors; the use of the Socratic method in questions and explanation of student outcomes; appropriate and varied methods to achieve goals and objectives; providing encouragement and feedback; basing tests on what was taught; helping students to reconstruct the information they learned; using varied teaching strategies such as using technology, and multi-sensory modalities; using assessments (alternative and traditional) that are based on state/district and teacher criteria; and displaying evidence of children's work and success (North Glade Elementary, n.d.).

A unit's philosophy might be construed, therefore, as its perspective on teaching and learning.

This perspective, gives direction to how unit faculty goes about teaching, the faculty's expected outcomes for candidates, and provides the philosophical justification for both. Pratt cautions, however, that a perspective on teaching and learning should not be confused with methods of teaching: "... the same teaching actions are common across perspectives.... It is how they are used, and toward what ends, that differentiates between perspectives" (Pratt, n.d).

Translating Philosophical Aim through Curricular Means

John Dewey maintains that "to have an aim is to act with meaning, not like an automatic machine; it is to *mean* to do something and to perceive the meaning of things in the light of that intent" (Dewey, 1944, 104). In fact, Dewey notes that "To have a mind to do a thing is to foresee a future possibility; it is to have a plan for its accomplishment; it is to note the means which make the plan capable of execution and the obstructions in the way ... it is to have a plan which takes account of resources and difficulties" (Dewey, 1916/1944, p. 103).

The philosophy of the unit thus enables one to understand how the unit uses its underlying beliefs - its philosophy of education - to direct its action in making educational decisions about what to teach and how to teach it through an articulated aim, that is, the unit's reason for existence.

According to the foregoing, a unit's conceptual framework, in particular the unit's aim or purpose, acts as the stimulation of a unit ethos within which continuous improvement, renewal, and change can occur. Units technically do not have aims. It is the collective persons in the unit that have aims. Therefore, as Dewey points out an aim is not an abstract idea but "... is of value so far as it assists observation, choice, and planning in carrying on activity from moment to moment and hour to hour" (Dewey, 1944, p. 107).

John Dewey notes that:

> ... an end which grows up within an activity as plan for its direction is always both ends and means, the distinction being only one of convenience. Every means is a temporary end until we have attained it. Every end becomes a means of carrying activity further as soon as it is achieved. We call it end when it marks off the future direction of the activity in which we are engaged; means when it marks off the present direction.

Every divorce of end from means diminishes by that much the significance of the activity and tends to reduce it to a drudgery from which one would escape if he could .... The educator, like the farmer, has certain things to do, certain resources with which to do, and certain obstacles with which to contend .... His aim is simply to utilize these various conditions; to make his activities and their energies work together, instead of against one another (Dewey, 1916/1944, p. 106).

According to Dewey (1944), an "... aim ... is experimental, and hence constantly growing as it is tested in action" (105):

The aim as it first emerges is a mere tentative sketch. The act of striving to realize its worth. If it suffices to direct activity successfully, nothing more is required, since its whole function is to set a mark in advance; and at times a mere hint may suffice. But usually--at least in complicated situations—acting upon it brings to light conditions which had been overlooked. This calls for revision of the original aim; it has to be added to and subtracted from (Dewey, 1944, 104).

Nicholas Burbules (2004) writing in *Educational Researcher* helps us grasp the concept and implication of an aim this way:

... this means deconstructing the means/ends dichotomy at the heart of the instrumentalist world view: that defining one's aims and purposes is one thing, and then deciding on effective means for achieving them is something else. This instrumentalist notion subverts questions of practice under an overarching discourse of effectiveness and efficiency. What Dewey's view challenges us to see, instead, is how selections of means (practices) constitute and are constituted by implicit assumptions about purposes and ends, each in turn modifying the other. If you think test scores are the indicia of educational quality, you will tend to teach in certain ways; but if you are required to teach in certain ways, it is equally true that you will be more likely to begin viewing test scores as the measure of your success. To a significant degree, our choice of methods determines our ends (and not only, as we usually think, vice versa).
... we need some way of counteracting the 'blinders effect,' where the pursuit of certain aims, however valuable they might be, makes us less attuned to the other, secondary or indirect, effects our actions may also have (p. 8).

An aim may, therefore, be construed as a stimulus to intelligent action in the unit through curricular and other means.

A unit's educational aim should, therefore, emerge out of the educational languages of general education, content studies, professional and pedagogical studies, and field and clinical studies. If education is seen as "the continued capacity for growth" then a unit's aim might be to produce the best possible leaders in education – persons who can continue to grow after graduation, become lifelong learners, and give service to others.

Moral Life in the Unit through Curricular Means

So how ought persons to live in the unit? Or in other words, how the curriculum might be used to help persons in the unit acquire the necessary moral sensibilities. A salient question thus becomes what is the curriculum supposed to accomplish? It is clear that without purpose, without being guided by an aim and goals/outcomes, curriculum becomes an end in and of itself. If that becomes the reality, then teachers standardize students. Peggy Maki (2002) cautions that:

> an institution has to assure itself that it has translated its mission and purposes into its programs and services to more greatly assure that students have opportunities to learn and develop what an institution values .... Without ample opportunity to reflect on and practice desired outcomes, students will not likely transfer, build upon, or deepen the learning and development an institution or program values (p. 10).

A graphic organizer for the foregoing idea is captured below:

SO HOW OUGHT YOU LIVE IN THE UNIT?

- Vision   ⟸⟹   What ought to be
- Philosophy
- Learning to
Live that Way   ⟸⟹   Acquiring moral
  - Outcomes/proficiencies   sensibilities
  - Standards Alignment
- Unit Programs
- Unit Operations

David Hansen points us in the direction of how we might bring curriculum alive so that candidates may acquire appropriate moral sensibilities. Drawing on Oakeshott (1989), Hansen states:

> According to Oakeshott, teachers initiate students into what he calls 'inheritances' and 'achievements' of humanity (pp. 22, 29-30, 41). He also calls them 'languages' in which human beings have historically sought to understand themselves: who they are, why they are here, how to conduct themselves, how to realize whatever possibilities the human condition makes available. For Oakeshott, the languages of poetry, art, philosophy, science, history, and so forth constitute something other than prescribed bodies of fact and information, although the latter play an indispensable role in helping students make their way into the world. Rather to enter these languages is to enter a field of human adventures (pp. 23, 26-28), one that features questions of meaning, understanding, and purpose rather than hardened answers or conclusions.
>
> This view of the curriculum carries us beyond narrow claims about 'cannons.' Such claims presuppose that the curriculum is purely a matter of adopting or supporting preexistent understandings rather than, for example, a matter of helping students grasp what it means to understand something in the first place.

To be sure, many teachers and administrators, from preschool through university, have acted as if the curriculum was supposed to dictate beliefs and outlooks, just as many teachers and administrators have failed to be attentive, thoughtful, and mindful of the significance of their work. But these failures underscore, among other things, the very real challenges in teaching well and in bringing curriculum alive (Hansen, 2001, pp.59-60).

If subject matter is construed as "... languages in which people, over the generations, have contemplated and questioned who they are, what they know, what they have done, how to lead a humane and flourishing life, and more" (Hansen, 2001, p. 84), then education enables one "... to enter [those] languages, expand one's horizons, and participate in the ongoing human conversation" (Hansen, 2001, p. 84).

Such an educational encounter means according to Hansen (2001) that all parties involved, teacher, student, and the subject matter, never remain the same as a result. This is so because, according to Hansen (2001), cognitive connections made through the acquisition of information (from the subject that is experienced), and technical intellectual skill (method – how the subject is experienced), influence the formation of social dispositions or "moral sensibilities" (habits accrued from the experience) In other words, meaning and states of mind or dispositions emerge from the transaction between subject and method. Accordingly, "the acquisition of dispositions is inherent in the process of education" (Sockett, 2004).

The moral life in the unit may thus be enhanced through curricular means if the unit takes into consideration the content of the curriculum (the relationship of general education, specialty studies, professional and pedagogical studies, and field and clinical experiences) as a means for candidates to (a) acquire cognitive knowledge through academic study (transmission), (b)   acquire process knowledge, i.e., skills, concerning professional practices and methods of inquiry (transaction), and (c) demonstrate "moral sensibilities" (Hansen, 2001) as reflected in professional values, ethics and commitments (transformation).

Candidates may, therefore, acquire depth and breadth of knowledge in languages, math, sciences, history, philosophy, literature, and the arts (general education); acquire knowledge of their respective fields of study, the structure of the respective field, the skills, competencies, concepts, ideas and values of the field (specialty studies); acquire knowledge of the social, historical and philosophical foundations of education; theories of human development; principles of effective practice; use of technology; evaluation/inquiry/research;

and educational policy and related processes/skills of independent thinking, effective communications, relevant judgments, professional collaboration, effective participation in educational system, skills in setting goals, developing curriculum, planning and managing instruction, instructional techniques, design/use of evaluation and assessment techniques, instructional strategies for exceptionalities, skills in the use of instructional technology, collaborative and consultative skills, and classroom and time management skills (professional and pedagogical).

Knowing something plus the relevant methods used to get to know something thus leads to transformation in disposition. The interaction of the foregoing that facilitates the demonstration of "moral sensibilities" (Hansen, 2001), or "habits of mind" (Costa & Kallick, 2000) is best captured by John Dewey this way. Dewey asks us to think of the process of eating in which the food is the content to be eaten, digestion is the method whereby the food is used, and taste (manners), the social disposition, emerges from and is acquired from the process of eating and digestion. To Dewey, to speak of the social disposition of taste outside of the food content and method is not an intelligent action (Dewey, 1916/1944).

The foregoing may be thought of as making cognitive connections. Consequently, the process Dewey outlined may be juxtaposed with the process of teaching and learning:

Cognitive Connections		
Process of Eating		Process of Teaching/learning
Food	[content]	Knowledge (teaching that something is the case)
Digestion	[method]	Skills (teaching how to do something)
Taste	[dispositions]	Moral sensibilities (tendencies toward patterns of intelligent action)

The "habits that render our action [conduct] intelligent" (Dewey, 1916/1944, p. 344) enhance our growth through the application of our thinking to things already known for the purpose of improving social conditions. Hansen (2001) suggests that these habits include: straightforwardness, open-mindedness, integrity of purpose, responsibility, simplicity, spontaneity, and naiveté. On the other hand, Costa and Kallick (2000) identify the following habits as applicable to adults and students who are engaged in effective problem solving and continuous learning: persisting, managing impulsivity, listening with understanding and empathy, thinking flexibly, thinking about thinking (metacognition), striving for accuracy, questioning and posing problems, applying past knowledge to new situations, thinking and communicating with clarity and precision, gathering data through all senses, creating, imagining, innovating, responding with wonderment and awe, taking responsible risks, finding humor, thinking interdependently, remaining open to continuous learning.

Tishman and Andrade (n.d.) call our attention to seven key critical thinking dispositions: to be broad and adventurous, a disposition toward sustained intellectual curiosity, to clarify and seek understanding, to be planful and strategic, to be intellectual and careful, to seek and evaluate reasons, and to be metacognitive.

On the other hand, Dewey (1916/1944) reminds us "Certain traits of character have such an obvious connection with our social relationships that we call them 'moral' in an emphatic sense – truthfulness, honesty, chastity, amiability, etc. " (p. 357). So if "... character and mind are attitudes of participative response in social affairs," (Dewey, 1916/1944, pp. 316-317 then Hansen is correct in asserting that "A moral sensibility embodies a person's disposition toward life and the people and events he or she encounters. It describes how a person fuses humaneness and thought in the way he or she regards and treats others" (Hansen, 2001, p. 32). In other words: "To be a student of students means developing the skills of moral perception, insight, and understanding that help the teacher fashion [an] educative environment" (Hansen, 2001, p. 67). To do so would entail the acquisition of social and emotional dispositions such as caring, trusting, supporting, and being compassionate, and so on. That means, that for moral education to be effective in a unit, it must cultivate opportunities for candidates to think about how their behavior affects those with whom they come, or will come into contact.

That is why Max van Manen's reference to the tact that brings "pedagogical thoughtfulness" is critical to the development of moral sensibilities in the professional educator (van Manen, 1991).

Desired Learning Outcomes/The Educative Process

The acquisition of "moral sensibilities" is not, therefore, a matter of ingesting subject matter. In fact, Tishman, Jay, and Perkins (1992) remind us that:

> Teaching by transmission treats as incidental matters [what] teaching by enculturation treats as part and parcel of the process. For instance, if you job as a teacher is to transmit a message to use meta-cognitive strategies and tactics, it matters little whether you yourself try to live up to that message. But if your aim is to acculturate in students an active commitment to meta-cognitive thinking, then it makes all the difference in the world. When teaching by enculturation, the tacit messages of the teacher's behavior, the physical space of the classroom, the tenor of classroom interactions, the standards and expectations exhibited, all become important. ... the transmission model is useful in some instances, particularly instances of direct instruction. But as a stand-alone model to guide teaching for thinking dispositions, it is simply too narrow. The transmission model is not rejected by the enculturation model but rather is included in it (p. 7).

Rick Weissbourd (2003) asserts that:

> ... moral qualities are shaped. Adults do not simply transmit moral qualities and beliefs to children. These qualities and beliefs emerge and continually evolve in the wide array of relationships that every child has with both adults and peers starting nearly at birth, and in children's felt knowledge of what is harmful, true, or right. In these relationships, children continually sort out, for example, what they owe others, what they should stand for, what traditions are worth keeping, whether to follow rules, how to contribute to their family, classroom, and community – in other words, how to be a decent human being (pp. 7-8).

If Weissbourd (2003) is correct then the educative process becomes the salient ground for moral development. In fact, John Dewey (1916/1944) notes:

... the only way in which adults consciously control the kind of education which the immature get is by controlling the environment in which they act and hence think and feel. We never educate directly, but indirectly by means of the environment. Whether we permit chance environments to do the work, or whether we design environments for the purpose makes a great difference.

And any environment is a chance environment so far as its educative influence is concerned unless it has been deliberately regulated with reference to its educative effect (p. 18).

To create a culture, in a unit, that facilitates the acquisition of "moral sensibilities" is contingent upon candidates seeing the disposition (exemplars), being able to interact with others in a manner that fosters the disposition (interaction with others), receiving direct instruction on the disposition (explanation and understanding), and having opportunities to receive feedback regarding the disposition (Tishman, Jay & Perkins, 1992).

A unit must, therefore, lay out in its conceptual framework the kind of educative process and environments the unit expressly intends to use to influence the intellectual and social dispositions of its candidates. In this process, a critical assumption is "... that the habits of life and intercourse which prevail are chosen, or at least colored, by the thought of their bearing upon the development of [candidates]" (Dewey, 1916/1944, p, 19). If a unit's goal is the educational growth of its candidates then it must recognize that the acquisition of certain habits must be seen as the background of that growth, and that such growth involves the candidates' thoughts, feelings and behaviors. In other words, education in this kind of educative process must be organized in a manner that enlists the natural active tendencies of candidates in their doing something (example, teaching, counseling, etc.). This doing, however, requires observation, the acquisition of information, and the use of the candidates' imagination so as to improve social conditions (the school, society, etc.).

To help candidates grow, the unit must, therefore, provide an educative environment in which candidates, faculty, administrators, and others in the unit acquire and demonstrate knowledge, relevant intellectual skills, and dispositions, or as put by Hansen (2001), "a growing person [embodies] moral traits... toward thinking and acting in the world (p. 44).

Acting in the world of professional practice is impacted by the reality that for all professions, certain moral attributes are absolutely essential for effective professional practice.

These moral attributes are usually delineated in Codes of Ethics which specify the criteria of good and bad conduct in the profession.

The unit's *aim,* therefore, is to produce professionals, who can engage in intelligent action, that is, demonstrate wisdom in practice, i.e., "pedagogical thoughtfulness." Consequently, the desired learning environment in the unit must facilitate for candidates (a) what is experienced – the subject matter, (b) how the subject matter is experienced – the method, and (c) the habits accrued from the experience. The foregoing may be captured in the unit as **outcomes of content, outcomes of processes,** and **outcomes of dispositions** (Costa & Garmston, 1998).

If the unit assumes that meaning will emerge for candidates from the transaction between content and processes then the **institutional standard** becomes that of ensuring that neither faculty, candidates, nor subject matter remain the same as a result of the encounter. So the learning outcomes for all in the unit are (1) the concepts and understandings candidates must have in their respective fields of study – the content outcome, (2) the requisite skills needed to be able to apply the concepts and understandings – the process outcome, and (3) the habits of mind that candidates will demonstrate as evidence of their growth – the dispositions outcome.

When the institutional standards for candidate learning are framed by content, process and disposition outcomes then it becomes much easier for the unit to answer the salient question, (did the candidates learn?), by showing that the candidates know more, can do some things better, and are more aware of their habits of mind. The moral development of candidates may then be linked to the learning process by which and in which candidates come to accept the unit's institutional standards, that is, the meaning derived from the candidates' use of subject and processes to emerge as a transformed professional.

Institutional standards thus become the unit's criteria used to judge the worth of candidate learning, and as such, learning outcomes (institutional standards) function to direct the unit's actions by providing a lens or focus as the unit engages in the process of education. These learning outcomes, therefore, establish a framework for subsequent decisions in the unit vis-à-vis what is taught and how it is taught.

Learning outcomes, therefore, describe the characteristics of the way of life the unit envisions for its graduates. These characteristics may also be construed of as **institutional standards** if standards are defined as normative positions of what should be.

For every learning outcome, that is, institutional standard, identified by a unit there should be good reasons or evidence for believing that a candidate's way of life in teaching or other professional roles ought to be that way.

Robert Fitzgibbons (1981) provides poignant advice regarding social outcomes of education. Writing in his book, *Making Educational Decisions: an Introduction to the Philosophy of Education,* Fitzgibbons suggests that in making decisions about social outcomes that a teacher education unit should identify characteristics that it thinks its candidates ought to possess. Fitzgibbons goes on to recommend that a unit should examine what the unit presently believes about salient candidate characteristics to determine what should be preserved, modified or eliminated. In so doing, Fitzgibbons maintains that a unit may come to realize that there are characteristics that the unit wants for its candidates but it does not have presently.

Of course, the image in mind of the characteristics the candidates' way of life ought to have should be consistent with the unit's vision or desired future. Marilyn King (1988) notes:

> To accomplish any lofty goal, you must have a crystal clear image of that goal and keep it uppermost in your mind. We know that by maintaining that image, the 'how-to' steps necessary for the realization of the goal will begin to emerge spontaneously. If you cannot imagine the goal, the 'how-to' steps will never emerge, and you'll never do it. Clearly the first step to any achievement is to dare to imagine that you can do it (n. p).

Lynn Stoddard, writing in *Redesigning Education: a Guide for Developing Human Greatness* (1992), operationalizes this outcomes process by showing that keeping a vision in mind contributed to the development of master goals (outcomes) for human greatness. According to Stoddard (1992), once one identifies the master goals one has good reason to believe a student's way of life ought to include then what follows is the need to determine whether teaching students some curriculum is both necessary and sufficient for the acquisition of those master goals, and, consequently what are the best assessment and evaluative tools for helping to determine what is to be accomplished.

Put another way, to generate learning outcomes, a unit may begin by considering the present realities in professional education and identify teaching and learning characteristics it deems as good.

Conversely, the unit may also identify teaching and learning characteristics it deems as not so good. The unit can then project the way of life it sees for its graduates, some five to ten years in advance (i.e., the beliefs and knowledge the candidate should possess, the skills he/she should demonstrate, and thoughts, behaviors and emotional attachments - dispositions - he/she should evince). It is this way of life that should characterize the outcomes for current unit candidates.

So, for example, a unit might determine that a candidate's way of life ought to possess the following: being a critical thinker, a responsive educator, a reflective practitioner, an instructional leader, a problem solver, a self-directed professional and an ethical truth seeker (Azusa Pacific University, California). A unit may then solicit confirmation of its learning outcomes from its professional community (the levels of agreement or disagreement with) by developing a survey in which each of the learning outcomes are identified and feedback sought on two dimensions regarding the characteristics that every candidate in the unit should evince in his/her professional life. Members of the unit's professional community might be asked, regarding each outcome, (a) whether current candidate graduates demonstrate the characteristic(s) or outcome(s), and (b) whether candidate graduates ought to demonstrate the characteristic(s) or outcome(s) in his/her professional life.

But since the aim of the unit is to move its community toward common ends of educational growth, then the unit must place the characteristics it deems necessary for the way of life of its candidates into the components of the educative process. As stated previously, the *aim* is to produce professionals, who can engage in intelligent action, that is, demonstrate wisdom in practice. Consequently, the desired learning environment in the unit must facilitate for candidates (a) what is experienced – the subject matter, (b) how the subject matter is experienced – the method, and (c) the habits accrued from the experience. The foregoing may be captured in the unit as **outcomes of content, outcomes of processes,** and **outcomes of dispositions** (Costa & Garmston, 1998).

The unit whose initial outcomes are critical thinker, responsive educator, reflective practitioner, instructional leader, problem solver, self-directed professional and ethical truth seeker might then accommodate these accordingly as content outcomes, process outcomes and outcomes of dispositions:

Content Outcome
Competent in content knowledge – instructional leader
Process Outcome
Reflective in practice – critical thinker, reflective practitioner, problem solver
Dispositions Outcome
Moral inquirer – responsive educator, self-directed professional and ethical truth seeker.

If it is remembered that the purpose of acquiring subject matter knowledge and of technical intellectual skill is to influence the formation of a social disposition (Dewey, 1916/1944), then the focus for candidates in all programs in the unit is on:

1. The acquired habits of intelligent action to deal with subject, people, and events (dispositions toward, life, people and events).
2. The knowledge to be learned (understand subject matter language)
3. The means by which candidates are engaged in the subject (skills and process to enhance wisdom in practice)

Tishman, Jay and Perkins (1992) capture the foregoing this way:

Can you play the piano? Do you play the piano? These are different questions, and your answers may well be 'yes' to the first and 'no' to the second. The first question asks about ability .... The second tacitly asks much more – it goes beyond ability and asks about inclination: Are you disposed to play the piano? ....
    While acknowledging that skills [and content knowledge] are important, this paper goes beyond a skills-centered view and proposes a dispositional approach .... We join the voices of others in stressing the importance of dispositions... and make the strong claim that being a good thinker *means* having the right thinking dispositions (p. 2).

The importance of acquired habits of intelligent action is also reinforced by Baron (1985) in his model of rationality. To Baron, cognitive capacities determine what a person can do, while dispositional factors determine what a person does do within the limits of those capacities.

Outcomes for Initial and Advanced Programs

So can there be common unit outcomes for both initial and advanced preparation programs? The Glossary of NCATE Terms indicates the following:

> **Advanced Preparation.** Programs at post-baccalaureate levels for (1) the continuing education of teachers who have previously completed initial preparation or (2) the preparation of other professional school personnel. Advanced preparation programs commonly award graduate credit and include master's, specialist, and doctoral degree programs as well as non-degree licensure programs offered at the graduate level.
> **Initial Teacher Preparation.** Programs at baccalaureate or post baccalaureate levels that prepare candidates for the first license to teach (NCATE, 2002, p. 52, 54).

Obviously, programs at the initial and advanced levels are different in degree if not in kind in some places. That being the case, some might suggest that characteristics that candidates in the different level programs ought to possess must be different. However, all programs, regardless of level, are interested in content, process and dispositions outcomes. What will differ among these programs and levels are the respective proficiencies for candidates and the degree of execution of those proficiencies.

For example, suppose a unit decides that the kinds of graduates it wants to develop are academic leaders, exemplary professionals who can facilitate learning, and ethical inquirers (Millersville University, Pennsylvania). It would seem impossible for any program in the unit, regardless of level not to be linked to those outcomes. That is, a candidate in an initial preparation program or a candidate in an advanced educational leadership program can be prepared to be an academic leader, an exemplary professional and an ethical inquirer.

One candidate will translate these outcomes as a classroom teacher; the other candidate will translate the outcomes in an educational leadership capacity. The content and process proficiencies to acquire those outcomes, however, will certainly be different in degree and kind.

Knowledge Base(s)

The justification offered for particular ways of life in teaching or other professional roles in schools should emerge from the knowledge base on teaching and learning and other professional roles in schools, for example, administration, counseling, and so on. In other words, each learning outcome identified by a unit should be justified as a reasonable way of life in teaching or other professional roles through theoretical knowledge, contemporary research, or the wisdom of practice as delineated in the current knowledge base literature (Murray, 1996; Reynolds, 1989; Richardson, 2001; Wittrock, 1986). This knowledge base enables a unit to justify not only the purpose for having its outcomes, but also the reasons for teaching candidates certain things and in certain ways so that they might come to possess the outcomes and therefore have a greater impact on P-12 student learning.

Lee Shulman (1987), for example, identified three types of knowledge base(s) for expert teaching: knowledge of the subject to be taught (content knowledge), knowledge of how to take the content and help others understand it (pedagogical-content knowledge), and knowledge of the general variety that includes how to motivate students, how to manage groups of students in a classroom setting, how to design and administer performance assessments, and so on (pedagogical knowledge).

On the other hand, the work of Wilson, Floden and Ferrini-Mundy (2001) provides a body of research related to teacher preparation that can provide justification for unit outcomes. For example, Wilson, Floden and Ferrini-Mundy (2001) found, among other things, the following: that there is a positive connection between subject matter preparation (content knowledge) and teacher performance; that pedagogical preparation positively affects teaching practice and student learning; that student teaching preparation is extremely powerful.

The foregoing research thus forms the knowledge base that should enable the unit to articulate the most current literature (empirical, theoretical, wisdom of practice) that supports why certain content, skills and abilities, and dispositions outcomes are relevant for success as a teacher or other school personnel.

Dottin (2001) maintains that:

> For every learning outcome, that is, institutional standard, identified by a unit there should be good reasons or evidence for believing that a candidate's way of life in teaching or other professional roles ought to be that way. The justification offered for particular ways of life in teaching or other professional roles in schools should emerge from the knowledge base on teaching and learning and other professional roles in schools, for example, administration, counseling, and so on. In other words, each learning outcome identified by a unit should be justified as a reasonable way of life in teaching or other professional roles though theoretical knowledge, contemporary research, or the wisdom of practice as delineated in the current knowledge base literature (Murray, 1996; Reynolds, 1989; Wittrock, 1986). This knowledge base enables a unit to justify not only the purpose for having its outcomes, but also the reasons for teaching candidates certain things and in certain ways so that they might come to possess the outcomes and therefore have a greater impact on P-12 student learning (p. 24).

So is there empirical justification in your unit's conceptual framework for the relationship between being an effective teacher, administrator, counselor, etc. and possessing academic scholarship, professional and pedagogical leadership, and democratic citizenship?

A measure of continuous improvement in a unit is the degree to which, from time to time, it reexamines its outcomes, and its justification for those outcomes, that is, the knowledge base for the learning outcomes.

Candidate Proficiencies

So what is the means by which the unit will help candidates to acquire the "moral sensibilities" it deems relevant to how life ought to be lived in the unit and in the world of practice? Let us first revisit the graphic representation of the foregoing:

SO HOW OUGHT YOU LIVE IN THE UNIT?

- Vision   ⟸⟹   What ought to be
- Philosophy
- Learning to
  Live that Way   ⟸⟹   Acquiring moral
  - Outcomes/proficiencies   sensibilities
  - Standards Alignment
- Unit Programs
- Unit Operations

According to the NCATE Standards (2002), the conceptual framework should identify "candidate proficiencies that are aligned with the expectations in professional, state, and institutional standards" (p. 12).

Candidate proficiencies provide an understanding of what candidates should know (knowledge), what they should be able to do (skills) and to what they should be disposed (dispositions). Since aims give rise to results, then this element of the conceptual framework should describe the learning outcomes for candidates - the institutional standards by which candidate learning, including the effect of candidate learning on P-12 student learning/performance, will be assessed.

The only kinds of things that can be taught regardless of subject categories are propositions (beliefs and understandings), skills, and dispositions. According to Fitzgibbons (1981) teaching a person a proposition amounts to teaching that something is the case:

> X can teach proposition P to Z such that Z understands P but does not believe that P is true. For example, the person might understand the proposition ['intuition is an instrument of knowledge'] but afford no psychological assent to it. Affording no psychological assent does not imply that Z believes that P is false (p. 185).

Fitzgibbons also notes that having a skill is having the ability to do something:

> If someone has a skill then he/she must actually be able to demonstrate it. [Frequent failure to do so is good reason to believe that he/she does not have the skill] (Fitzgibbons, 1981, p. 186).

So, teaching a person a skill amounts to teaching a person how to do something:

> Teaching skill S to Z amounts to behaving in such a way that Z acquires the ability to do S. Assuming that no previous possession of the skill, Z's degree of proficiency at S is increased from none at all to some. If Z already possessed skill S to some degree then teaching skill S to Z amounts to increasing Z's proficiency to a higher level (Fitzgibbons, 1981, p. 188).

Fitzgibbons also points out that a disposition is a tendency to do something:

> To fully describe a particular disposition of a person you have to specify not only what is done, but the conditions under which it is done and the regularity with which the person does it under those conditions. Just how often the person does it when the conditions hold determines the strength of his/her disposition (Fitzgibbons, 1981, p. 188).

Since teaching is not just a matter of applying technical expertise to fixing problems, but involves "tact and pedagogical thoughtfulness" (van Manen, 1991), then the unit programs and its operations must play a vital role in helping candidates to acquire the necessary tact and pedagogical thoughtfulness. According to Maki (2002) "An institution has to assure itself that it has translated its [vision], mission and purposes [philosophy] into its programs and services to more greatly assure that [candidates] have opportunities to learn and develop what an institution values.... Without ample opportunity to reflect on and practice desired outcomes, [candidates] will not likely transfer, build upon, or deepen the learning and development an institution or program values (p. 10). Of course, the desired outcomes are manifested in the subject or content to be experienced, the requisite methods for experiencing the content, and the dispositions (moral sensibilities) inherent in the transaction of the foregoing.

The unit's values may, therefore, be operationalized through three major outcomes: (1) The acquisition of content/subject knowledge, (2) the acquisition of professional knowledge and skills necessary to be able to apply the content/subject knowledge, and (3) the transformation characteristics inherent in (1) and (2). These are generic outcomes that candidates in ALL programs must pursue. The unit's desired future, its philosophy and aim thus engender its need to develop:

An Educational Leader – who is conversant with and understands subject matter language
A Reflective Practitioner – who engenders wisdom in practice
A Moral Pedagogue – who manifests tact and pedagogical thoughtfulness.

Since the justification for the above outcomes must come from the knowledge base of teacher education, it follows that this knowledge base should facilitate the manifestation of relevant candidate proficiencies for each outcome. For example, to be an educational leader who is conversant with and understands specific subject matter language, the knowledge base might point to the acquisition of content knowledge and pedagogical content knowledge. Likewise, the knowledge base may point to certain professional and pedagogical knowledge and skills needed to be a reflective practitioner, and to certain habits of mind germane to being a moral pedagogue. The foregoing may be captured as follows:

| UNIT OUTCOMES |
| KNOWLEDGE BASE(S) JUSTIFICATION |

If the unit and its programs are to work toward the generic outcomes then eventual expectations for candidate learning must be delineated. These expectations are **candidate proficiencies.** These proficiencies or **institutional standards** which are framed by the knowledge base in the unit's conceptual framework capture the desired candidate learning and development. As a result, these proficiencies must be described through active verbs that capture the desired learning and development (e.g., design, create, analyze, etc.). The building blocks for **institutional standards** may be construed as below:

UNIT OUTCOMES
KNOWLEDGE BASE(S) JUSTIFICATION

CANDIDATE PROFICIENCIES (from knowledge base)
Knowledge, Skills, Dispositions

For example, a unit may find that to achieve the outcome of an educational leader who is conversant with and understands subject language, its candidates must know the facts and principles of the subject matter in his/her field of study, and consequently, must know and can demonstrate how to assist students in the mastery of content in his/her field of study. Conversely, to achieve the outcome of a reflective practitioner, the unit might find that the knowledge base suggests the candidates must know and can demonstrate how to facilitate solutions to problems. To enhance candidates' being moral pedagogues, the unit might find that candidates must be committed to caring for others.

Now the building of institutional standards may be seen accordingly:

UNIT OUTCOMES
KNOWLEDGE BASE(S) JUSTIFICATION

CANDIDATE PROFICIENCIES (from knowledge base)
Knowledge, Skills, Dispositions

INSTITUTIONAL STANDARDS
Three Major Unit Outcomes
Knowledge, Skills, Dispositions (for each major outcome)

Standards Alignment: Institutional, State and Professional Standards

The idea of a quality effectiveness continuum in professional education necessitates that quality assurance in a unit should be a matter of being guided by internal outcomes (institutional standards) that are congruent and aligned with state and professional standards. These standards include those disseminated by:

(1) the Interstate New Teacher Assessment and Support Consortium,
(2) the National Board for Professional Teaching standards, and
(3) subject specialty standards.

Since the professional education unit is a part of a quality assurance continuum, its way of seeing and thinking, its conceptual framework, must therefore explain its contribution to the authority which governs its existence, the State, and to the profession, as manifested in professional standards.

The unit's conceptual framework or meta-narrative thus provides an interpretation of how the unit moves from its performance learning outcomes, that is, its institutional standards, to its aligning these outcomes/institutional standards with performance outcomes promulgated in state and professional standards.

What will be aligned are candidate proficiencies; that is, the related knowledge, skills, and dispositions in institutional, state, and professional standards. As a result, a unit may identify a common core of essential candidate proficiencies for each of its three major outcomes and show alignment among these proficiencies (institutional standards) and state, INTASC and NBPTS Standards (see below):

Initial Level Programs

Institutional Standards (Unit Outcomes)	State Standards	INTASC Standards	NBPTS
Knowledge	Knowledge	Knowledge	Knowledge
Skills	Skills	Skills	Skills
Dispositions	Dispositions	Dispositions	Dispositions

Advanced Level Programs

Institutional Standards (Unit Outcomes)	State Standards	INTASC Standards	NBPTS
Knowledge	Knowledge	Knowledge	Knowledge
Skills	Skills	Skills	Skills
Dispositions	Dispositions	Dispositions	Dispositions

On the other hand, the unit's three major outcomes will be acquired and demonstrated in numerous and varied contexts based on the different initial and advanced level programs in the unit. Consequently, units should first establish that ALL programs are linked to the three major unit outcomes (transmission content outcome, transaction pedagogical outcome, and transformation in moral sensibilities outcome). Then each program (whether initial bachelor's, initial master's, advanced master's or advanced doctoral) may articulate the candidate proficiencies (consistent with the knowledge base for teacher education and the knowledge base for the specific program) for the three major outcomes that are unique to the program (see below).

PROGRAM
Unit Outcome (Content/Pedagogical Content)
Program Candidate Proficiencies

Unit Outcome (Professional & Pedagogical Knowledge and Skills)
Program Candidate Proficiencies

Unit Outcome (Dispositions)
Program Candidate Proficiencies

This process of conceptual development for the unit and its programs enables the unit to also conceptualize Standard 1 of the NCATE Standards (2002) in a manner consistent with unit and program outcomes. Standard 1 states that "Candidates preparing to work in schools as teachers or other professional school personnel know and demonstrate the content, pedagogical, and professional knowledge, skills, and dispositions necessary to help all students learn...." (NCATE Standards, p. 14). The unit and program outcomes and candidate proficiencies may thus be aligned with the elements in Standard 1 as shown below:

Program (Level)	NCATE Standard 1 Alignment
Outcome (Subject matter understanding)	
Candidate Proficiencies A B C	Standard 1 – Elements Content Knowledge for Teacher Candidates or Content Knowledge for Other School Personnel Pedagogical Content for Teacher Candidates
Outcome (Wisdom in practice)	
Candidate Proficiencies A B C	Standard 1 – Elements Professional and Pedagogical Knowledge and Skills for Teacher Candidates or Professional Knowledge and Skills for Other School Personnel
Outcome (Moral Sensibilities)	
Candidate Dispositions/Habits of Mind A B C	Standard 1 – Element Dispositions for all Candidates

It is the above proficiencies that will be used by teacher candidates and other school personnel to impact P-12 student learning (the final two elements of NCATE Standard 1).

This component of the conceptual framework now engenders a unit (through its programs) to explore the aspects of the candidate proficiencies in its institutional standards that are also in other standards (state, professional, etc.). It also enables the unit's programs to determine the courses and/or experiences that will facilitate candidates' acquisition of the proficiencies (see below).

Program (Level)	NCATE Standard 1 Alignment		
Outcome (Subject matter understanding)			
Candidate Proficiencies A B C	Standard 1 - Elements	Courses/Experiences	Aspects in professional and state standards
Outcome (Wisdom in practice)			
Candidate Proficiencies A B C	Standard 1 - Elements	Courses/Experiences	Aspects in professional and state standards
Outcome (Moral Sensibilities)			
Candidate Dispositions/Habits of Mind A B C	Standard 1 - Element	Courses/Experiences	Aspects in professional and state standards

It is the above unit and program candidate proficiencies that will be used by teacher candidates and other school personnel to impact P-12 student learning (the final two elements of NCATE Standard 1).

Maintaining an Evaluation/Assessment System
The System for Unit and Program Effectiveness

The final structural element of the conceptual framework delineates the results orientation and commitment to continuous improvement in the unit's professional community, in other words, unit and program effectiveness.

If the unit is moving conceptually from questions of purpose (why), to questions of content (what), to questions of delivery (how), then the crux of its evaluation system must entail its ascertaining whether graduates are acquiring the learning outcomes, that is, meeting the institutional standards, and as a result, whether it is achieving its overall aim. This element of the conceptual framework therefore provides answers to how the unit is achieving and when the unit has achieved its aim.

This element of the conceptual framework describes the extent to which the aim and outcomes as conceptually developed and organized, will produce and are actually producing the desired results.

In other words, this element of the conceptual framework should highlight:

(a) the active and meaningful participation of the unit's professional community in evaluative and assessment decisions that directly impact the continuous improvement of its programs.

(b) the system for the assessment and evaluation of candidate performance.

(c) the use of and means to valid and reliable internal and external unit operational data for improvement results and ongoing unit accountability.

The unit's evaluation and assessment systems should be structured conceptually to enable decisions to be made regarding whether the unit is achieving its aim and learning outcomes and therefore producing desired results. Evaluation and assessment must be conceptually constructed to show both elements being essential features of the unit's continuous development.

The conceptual framework as a way of seeing, thinking and being enables units to move from questions of purpose (why) to questions of content (what) to questions of method (how). The "when" of the unit's efforts is its assessment and evaluation system that enables it to ascertain whether its candidates and graduates are acquiring the unit's learning outcomes, and consequently whether the unit is achieving its overall aim, its purpose.

Once a unit has decided upon its purpose for existence, and how life ought to be lived in the unit, it must next decide what should be taught and learned in its programs to achieve that purpose. Units must ensure the following:

(1) that candidates demonstrate the dispositions and habits of mind that would render their actions more intelligent.

(2) That candidates know the subjects they will teach;

(3) and can demonstrate the knowledge and competence expected of beginning or experienced teachers or other school personnel.

A unit may utilize both internal and external evaluative checks of the foregoing.

On the other hand, the unit's use of a conceptual framework as a way of seeing and thinking facilitates its also seeing and thinking about requisite input processes such as the culture of the unit in terms of candidate and faculty composition and propensity to enrich diversity in the curriculum, etc.; faculty performance and development, that is, their scholarship of the classroom; the institutional and unit will to govern, and capacity to provide necessary resources and facilities.

The conceptual framework, therefore, facilitates evaluation and assessment to be seen and thought about on two levels: the unit and the individual candidate. The unit needs to know whether its graduates are mastering institutional, state and professional standards, and how related enablers such as unit culture, faculty performance, and so on are contributing to such success. The unit also needs to know whether each candidate is learning the content, professional and pedagogical knowledge, skills and dispositions appropriate to his/her field as demonstrated by the individual's performance. A unit may conceptualize the foregoing accordingly:

Assessment of Candidate Proficiencies	Evaluation of Unit Operations

The assessment of candidate proficiencies would require that a unit:

1. Is able to offer conceptual justification for why candidate performance is assessed the way it is.

2. Delineates what is assessed? How is it assessed? When is it assessed? Who assesses it? What measures are used to determine validity and reliability of assessments? Who monitors the assessment system?

3. Lays out a timeline for the implementation and operation of the foregoing.

On the other hand, information about the unit's productivity, resources, and personnel is critical to the unit's evaluation of organizational level performance. The overall evaluation and assessment system may be captured accordingly:

	Programs	Unit
Internal	Candidate Performance Assessment	Resources Data Productivity Data Personnel Data
External	Candidate Performance on state and national exams	Graduates' Feedback Employers /Clinical Supervisors Evaluation

The unit's activity vis-à-vis its maintaining an evaluation/assessment system must enable it to answer the following questions:

Is there an overall assessment system in the unit to determine whether graduates are acquiring the unit's learning outcomes?
Does the system provide internal and external checks on candidates' performance?
Does the system provide internal and external unit operational data?
Does the system ensure assessment of goals progress and use of results in the unit's improvement process?
Does the system foster ongoing unit accountability?

The alignment of institutional, state, and professional standards may thus enable the unit and its programs to map out evidence of candidate learning vis-à-vis its outcomes and candidate proficiencies (see chart below):

Program (Level)	NCATE Standard 1 Alignment			
Outcome (Subject matter understanding)				
Candidate Proficiencies A B C	Standard 1 - Elements	Courses	Aspects in professional and state standards	Evidence of candidate learning
Outcome (Wisdom in practice)				
Candidate Proficiencies A B C	Standard 1 - Elements	Courses	Aspects in professional and state standards	Evidence of candidate learning
Outcome (Moral Sensibilities)				
Candidate Dispositions/Habits of Mind A B C	Standard 1 - Element	Courses	Aspects in professional and state standards	Evidence of candidate learning

A unit may ask each of its programs (initial and advanced) to use the above chart. The process would be consistent with, and help to facilitate the new Program Review process implemented by NCATE in 2004. After all programs have completed the above, then the unit should look across all programs at the different levels (initial, advanced) and cull out those assessments that are the most common across all programs for the major outcomes and proficiencies. For example, at the initial preparation level, a look across all programs at the subject matter understanding outcome might reveal that one of the proficiencies for that outcome might be that candidates demonstrate competency in their chosen content area.

A common assessment feature across all programs might be an exam
showing the candidate's understanding and/or results on an external
examination such as the PRAXIS (operated by the Educational Testing
Service of New Jersey). These assessments, and the results of these
assessments, would then become part of the unit's overall assessment
system, and of the program review process. These assessments and
their results would also serve as evidence of meeting the first element
in Standard 1 of the NCATE Standards (2002).
The foregoing may then be visualized as seen below:

Outcomes/ Proficiencies	Assessment Artifact(s)	Who or what does the Assessment?	Transition Point of Assessment	Rubric(s) – fairness, accuracy	Data – results and use
Know Field Proficiencies K-S-D	Exam Praxis II	Course(s) ETS	During Program Prior to Exit		

What is assessed? (outcomes/proficiencies); how is it assessed?
(artifacts); who assesses it? (instructors in courses, etc.); when is it
assessed? (at what points in the unit's transition, that is, curriculum
delivery system – pre-entry/admissions, the acquisition of content
knowledge, pedagogical content knowledge – initial and continuing
teachers, professional and pedagogical knowledge and skills – initial
and continuing teachers, and professional knowledge and skills – other
school personnel, helping all students learn in P-12 settings prior to
program exit – initial and continuing teachers, and creating positive
learning environments – other school personnel; are rubrics used? (Are
they checked for fairness, accuracy, etc.?); are data sampled and
summarized and are the results used to improve programs and the unit?
(continuous improvement).
A data collection format, at different transition points, on individual
candidates in the unit's programs may then be conceptualized
accordingly:

Potential for Success/Admission (Initial Preparation, Advanced Preparation)

Proficiencies assessed at pre-entry to program?				Scoring
	Level of performance – inadequate (1)	Level of performance – adequate (2)	Level of performance – outstanding (3)	
How are proficiencies assessed? (artifacts)				Performance points
				Total Points

Program Delivery (Initial Preparation, Advanced Preparation)

Proficiencies assessed in program?				Scoring
	Level of performance – inadequate (1)	Level of performance – adequate (2)	Level of performance – outstanding (3)	
How are proficiencies assessed? (artifacts)				Performance points
				Total Points

Field and Clinical Practice and Impact on P-12 Learning/Creating
Positive Learning Environment (Initial Preparation, Advanced
Preparation)

Proficiencies assessed in field and clinical practice				Scoring
	Level of performance – inadequate (1)	Level of performance – adequate (2)	Level of performance – outstanding (3)	
How are proficiencies assessed? (artifacts)				Performance points
				Total Points

The consequences for candidates performing at different levels may
thus emerge from the foregoing. This process is consistent with the
NCATE Unit Accreditation Board's Pre-Conditions Requisites
regarding the conceptual framework:

Precondition #4. The unit has a well developed conceptual
framework that establishes the shared vision for a unit's efforts in
preparing educators to work in P–12 schools and provides
direction for programs, courses, teaching, candidate performance,
scholarship, service, and unit accountability.
4.1 The vision and mission of the institution and unit.
4.2 The unit's philosophy, purposes, and goals.
4.3 Knowledge bases, including theories, research, the wisdom
of practice, and education policies, that informs the unit's
conceptual framework.
4.4 Candidate proficiencies aligned with the expectations in
professional, state, and institutional standards.
4.5 Summary of assessment system for assessing candidate
proficiencies in 4.4
- when candidates are assessed
- types of assessments

- how unit ensures assessments are accurate, and consistent
- consequences for candidates performing at different levels.

The relevance of the unit's conceptual framework as a way of thinking comes to the fore at this point. If the unit is to move "beyond just compliance" and focus on the moral end of its endeavor, then the assessments and related artifacts must be seen as social ends toward which candidates in learning communities will pursue. To do so, however, requires candidates making cognitive connections through the acquisition of intellectual and technical knowledge and skills, and, as a result, their being transformed (demonstrating moral sensibilities).

The unit's mindset regarding assessment of learning should not degenerate into modes of competency reductionism, but instead should be on using assessments to structure the learning environment to enable candidates to use the curriculum to establish cognitive connections in their respective subject areas, and consequently, acquire salient "pedagogical thoughtfulness." According to Arthur Costa,   "When teachers deliberately adopt and assess Habits of Mind, it changes the design of their activities, determines their selection of content and enlarges their assessments. The bigger the circle in which the outcomes live, the more influence they exert on the values of each habit" (file:///C:/Documents%20and%20Settings/Erskine%20S.%20Dottin/Desktop/habits.html).

Showing Long Term Goals Alignment

> The juxtaposition of vision (what we want) and a clear picture of current reality (where we are relative to what we want) generates ... 'creative tension'. Learning in this context does not mean acquiring more information, but expanding the ability to produce results we truly want in life. It is lifelong generative learning (Senge, 1990, 142).

VISION
Desired Future

AIM
Stimulus to intelligent action

DELIVERY OF CURRICULUM	STRATEGIC PLANNING Goals
Movement of subject knowledge toward ends	Referring present conditions to future results, and future consequences to present conditions

Peter Senge's notion of "creative tension" between what ought to be, one's vision or aim, and current organizational realities, what is, produces a needs index for change. This index may be translated through long term goals. Goals, in this context, may therefore be construed as mechanisms for planning for change. They create opportunities for short term successes or failures that fuel the change process. A long-term goal is therefore a general statement regarding what a unit would like to see happen and consequently long-term goals take time to accomplish.

The development of long term goals may emerge through different paths. For example, one goals development path emerges from vision to goals to achieve the vision (Peterson, 1995). Another example of goals development emerges from mission to goals to achieve the mission (many universities engaged in developing performance outcomes use this strategy).

The option proposed here emerges from the conceptual idea of a unit's long term goals being construed as means through which the unit's vision/theme, mission, and philosophy/aim are advanced.

In other words, the long-term goals become the steps through which evidence to demonstrate progress in a unit's aim is manifested (through plans, goals, objectives, timelines, and use of results for change and improvement). In this option, planning and evaluation (strategic planning) is given meaning through the conceptual framework in terms of what the unit delivers in order to achieve its aim. The goals become an extension of a unit's aim and therefore are not someone else's goals being adopted. Instead, they should reflect the unit's values, and sense of purpose. As noted by Senge (1990) "... nothing happens until there is vision. But it is equally true that a vision with no underlying sense of purpose, [aim] no calling, is just a good idea - all 'sound and fury, signifying nothing'" (149).

It is the identification and pursuit of explicit goals that foster the experimentation, results orientation, and commitment to continuous improvement that characterizes a unit's learning community.

Goals, therefore, foster ongoing accountability, and performance benchmarks become natural accountability indicators to measure progress and growth.

According to a former Dean of the College of Education at Florida International University, continuous improvement in a unit may be seen as a mechanism for enhancing institutional effectiveness:

> Strategic planning is the process through which a setting addresses itself to the issues of securing its future in a manner that is both consistent with its evolving identity, and inclusive of its stakeholders. Thus, it is an ongoing process that provides the community, and its members with the opportunity to regularly and continually assess two (2) critical issues: first, the degree to which the setting is approaching and/or achieving its stated goals; and second, the manner in which it must prioritize and allocate its resources if it is to increase the probability of actualizing its shared intentions.
>
> Both the process and product of strategic planning are embedded in a 'context,' a framework that serves to provide the setting with a sense of its own identity, purpose and uniqueness. In turn, this framework enables the planning process (and the resulting plan) to eventuate in more than a continuing exercise in rhetoric: it provides the setting with the basis for developing a manageable and realistic blueprint for its own future. At its very best, strategic planning offers a setting the possibility of utilizing the present as a point in time through which the past is celebrated and the future is welcomed (Personal Communication, Dean, I. Ira Goldenberg, January 27, 1996).

The context of continuous improvement that occurs within a conceptual framework establishes a way of thinking and a way of being that moves a unit to thinking in terms of the whole (the unit) to its parts (departments, programs, etc.), and back to the whole, the college or school of education. This "way of thinking" facilitates a unit's way of making meaning of its decisions in the following areas: the curriculum (how the curriculum is delivered), candidates (how the unit attends to candidates), faculty (how the unit enhances faculty vitality), and governance (how unit accountability is provided).

This framework for making moral meaning thus facilitates movement in seeking to enhance unit effectiveness from matters of purpose (why), to matters of content (what), to matters of method (how), to matters of assessment and evaluation (when – determining when the purpose has been achieved).

The unit's conceptual framework may thus give meaning to its "goals focused development" in terms of what is delivered in order to achieve its aim. This form of "goals focused development" thus leads to a model of the moral relationship between the college (the unit), its departments and programs, and the products and goals each develops in order to enhance a unified, and coherent professional community through means-ends connections to facilitate the acquisition of moral dispositions.

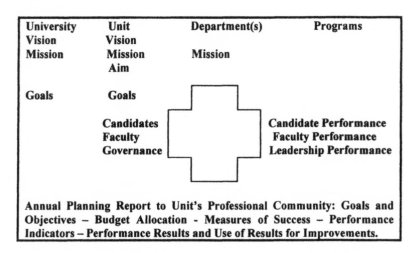

CHAPTER THREE

LIVING THE CONCEPTUAL FRAMEWORK

Living the Conceptual Framework

To live presuppose growth, consequently, for a unit to live its conceptual framework implies growth in the unit. To modify John Dewey's thoughts here, "The criterion of value of [the unit's conceptual framework] is the extent to which it creates a desire for continued growth [in the unit] and supplies means for making the desire effective in fact" (Dewey, 1916/1944, p. 53).

Growth in the unit, using Dewey's way of thinking:

> must progressively realize present possibilities, and thus make individuals better fitted to cope with later requirements. Growing is not something which is completed in odd moments; it is a continuous leading into the future. If the environment in school and out, supplies conditions which utilize adequately the present capacities of the immature, the future which grows out of the present is surely taken care of. The mistake is not in attaching importance to preparation for future need, but in making it the mainspring of present effort. Because the need of preparation for a continually developing life is great, it is imperative that every energy should be bent to making the present experience as rich and significant as possible. Then as the present merges insensibly into the future, the future is taken care of (Dewey, 1916/1944, p. 56).

If a conceptual framework, therefore, is to enhance growth, and is to enhance the making of moral judgments, and to provide and bring moral structure, coherence and consistency to experiences in a unit, then there must be continuous analysis of relationships among beliefs, between beliefs and actions, and relationships among actions. This process requires good thinking and the making of judgments.

According to John Dewey (1916/1944), "The most important problem of moral education in the school concerns the relationship of knowledge and conduct. For unless the learning which accrues in the regular course of study affects character, it is futile to conceive the moral end as the unifying and culminating end of education" (p. 360).

Living the Conceptual Framework: Beyond Compliance

Living the conceptual framework in the unit implies a sense of thinking and making judgments in the unit rather than simply complying with all external mandates. If one modifies the words of Lipman, Sharp and Oscanyan (1977) here then:

> Thinking ... [in the unit] involves a reflection upon [experiences in the unit] and upon [the unit's] own situation in the world. It requires appraisal of [the unit's] own values and in effect of [the unit's] own identity. It further involves a search for more and more reliable criteria so that the judgments [made] in the course of [the unit's] life rest upon a firm and solid foundation" (p. 14).

The foregoing authors also point out that:

> making ... judgments – involves developing a sense of personal direction toward the goals that one foresees, however dimly, for oneself. This is not to imply that the moral life is a journey by an individual with a fixed personal identity towards certain fixed and unalterable goals. It is rather that the ends which at any one time we hold to be desirable are held tentatively, and the self at any one time is always in a process of transition contingent upon the means that are available to use to achieve the goals that are sought.... The availability of means conditions and modifies our ideals and objectives, just as conversely, the ends we have in view control the way we search for means to employ, and the selves which we are in process of becoming (Lipman, Sharp and Oscanyan, 1977, p. 15).

Living the conceptual framework may be seen as a model of self renewal in a unit. In order for the unit to provide necessary educative opportunities to its members to learn and develop what is valued in the unit, the unit must live its conceptual framework by translating its vision, mission and philosophy through its programs and services in a manner that enables candidates to gain wisdom in practice.

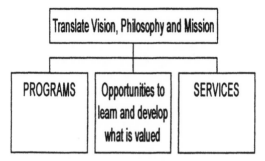

Having a sense of purpose is a catalyst for change. According to Fullan (1993):

> ... personal purpose is the route to *organizational* change. When personal purpose is diminished we see in its place groupthink and a continual stream of fragmented surface, ephemeral innovations. We see in a phrase, the uncritical acceptance of innovation, the more things change, the more they remain the same. When personal purpose is present in numbers it provides the power for deeper change (14).

If one perceives a conceptual framework as engendering a sense of unit purpose, then the more persons in the unit are committed to that purpose the greater the power for change. In fact, one may construe the essential activity for keeping a conceptual framework current as inquiry "the engine of vitality and self-renewal" (Pascale, 1990, 14). In other words, the relationship between the conceptual framework (unit purpose) and continuous improvement (inquiry) is "the ability to simultaneously *express and extend* what you value. The genesis of change arises from this dynamic tension" (Fullan, 1993, 15).

Living the conceptual framework is thus a form of creative tension between what is and what ought to be. According to Jones (1996) "People who focus mostly on 'what is' will create more of 'what is.' People who focus mostly on 'what could be' will begin to create 'what could be' "(p. 94).

So living the conceptual framework in the unit is for the purpose of achieving "like-mindedness" through the pursuit of common ends that are grounded in educative means, and supported by short and long-term unit effectiveness goals.

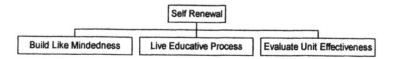

So improving life lived in common so the future will be better than the present becomes the salient feature of living the conceptual framework. In other words, to live the conceptual framework means to "... give guidance and regulation and direction to what would otherwise be a fluid and amorphous [unit] with no continuity and no sense of unit" (Lipman, Sharp and Oscanyan, 1977, p.15).

Living the conceptual framework should, therefore, be a demonstration of the unit's decision regarding how life ought to be lived in the unit. Moral conduct in the unit might thus be guided by thoughtfulness and reflection. This thoughtfulness and reflection, that is, making moral judgments, become a matter of developing a sense of the unit's direction towards its ends.

As Dewey (1916/1944) notes:

> A narrow and moralistic view of morals is responsible for the failure to recognize that all the aims and values which are desirable in education are themselves moral. Discipline, natural development, culture, social efficiency, are moral traits – marks of a person who is a worthy member of that society which it is the business of education to further. There is an old saying to the effect that it is not enough for a man to be good; he must be good for something. The something for which a man must be good is capacity to live as a social member so that what he gets from living with others balances with what he contributes. What he gets and gives as a human being, a being with desires, emotions, and ideas, is not external possessions, but a widening and deepening of conscious life - a more intense, disciplined, and expanding realization of meanings. What he *materially* receives and gives is at most opportunities and means for the evolution of conscious life (p. 359).

Working toward getting candidates, faculty, and staff in the unit to demonstrate habits of mind through wisdom in practice is, therefore, a moral endeavor: "What is learned and employed in an occupation having an aim and involving cooperation with others is moral knowledge, whether consciously so regarded or not" (Dewey, 1916/1944, p. 356).

Living the conceptual framework, therefore, induces attention to a means and ends connection:

Means-Ends Connections

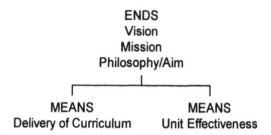

Conceptualizing Curricular Phenomena

If "standards" are interpreted as normative ends of what ought to be, then thinking in the unit, that is, using a conceptual framework, may be used to visualize and conceptualize what ought to be in the NCATE Standards. NCATE Standards are intended to assist units in their decision making. As noted by Robert Fitzgibbons (1981) all educational decisions made in an educational unit fall into one or another of three categories of, outcomes or the aims of the endeavor, content or what is or could be taught and learned, and methods or the ways in which some content is or could be taught.

Another way of looking at the foregoing is to recognize the following:

1. Educators have aims that motivate them and guide what they do (e.g., Plato's just society) - **WHY**.
2. Educators structure content knowledge in an attempt to serve certain aims (e.g., Gilbert Ryle's idea of knowing that and knowing how; Harry Broudy's idea of   replicative, associative, applicative and interpretive knowledge) - **WHAT**.

3. Educators propose ways for organizing and carrying out instruction that are rationally consistent with those aims (e.g., Alfred North Whitehead's idea of romance, precision and generalization; John Dewey's meaningful experiences; Jerome Bruner's discovery learning; William Kilpatrick's the project method) - **HOW**.

4. Educators seek to find out whether learning experiences are actually producing the desired results, that is, helping to achieve educational aims (e.g., Ralph Tyler's system for comparing actual accomplishments with stated objectives) - **WHEN**.

The NCATE Performance-Based Standards may, therefore, be conceptualized using the above markers.

Conceptualizing the NCATE Performance-Based Standards

THE WHY for the Unit and its Programs	Vision Mission Philosophy/Aim Learning Outcomes and Candidate Proficiencies Knowledge Base Alignment of Outcomes and Proficiencies with State and Professional Standards Why Performance is Assessed the Way it is
The structural elements of the conceptual framework	The structural elements of the conceptual framework

| THE WHAT that is taught and THE HOW of teaching and learning that is consistent with the unit's WHY

Standard 1 – Candidate Knowledge, Skills, and Dispositions
Standard 3 – Field Experiences and Clinical Practice
Standard 4 – Diversity (curricular experiences) | Content Knowledge
Pedagogical Content Knowledge
Professional and Pedagogical Knowledge
Dispositions
What teachers and other school personnel should know and be able to do in applying professional and pedagogical knowledge in clinical and school settings |

THE WHEN of the Unit's efforts to determine whether it is achieving its aim	Determining Candidate Performance and its Impact on P-12 Student Learning
Standard 2 – Assessment System and Unit Evaluation	

PERFORMANCE ENABLERS FOR CURRICULUM
Standard 4 – The Unit's Culture (working with diverse faculty, with diverse candidates, with diverse P-12 students)
Standard 5 – Faculty Qualifications, Performance and Development (qualifications, teaching, scholarship, service, collaboration, evaluation, and professional development)
Standard 6 – Institutional and Unit Will and Capacity (leadership – to enhance strategic planning and continuous improvement, budget, personnel – workload policies and means for improvement, facilities, and resources including technology)

Using the Conceptual Framework to Live the NCATE Standards

Rules tell us how to act or behave in certain contexts. A standard is a measure used to judge the worth of something. Consequently, according to Lipman and Sharp (1977): "One obeys a rule; one does not obey a standard. A standard is a criterion by means of which one can distinguish one kind of thing from another or tell the better from the worse" (p. 12). Living the unit's conceptual framework through the NCATE standards is, therefore, a process of making better judgments about how life ought to be lived in the unit. In other words, in living its conceptual framework, a unit's aim is to act with meaning and perceive the meaning of things in light of that intent vis-à-vis the performance of candidates, the performance of faculty, and the performance of unit governance.

Since the acquisition of meaning is linked to aims (Dewey, 1916/1944), then a unit to live its conceptual framework should use its ends (vision, philosophy and mission) to visualize the performance components of the NCATE Standards: candidate performance (standards 1, 2, 3, and 4), faculty performance (standard 5), and unit governance performance (standard 6).

Living the Conceptual Framework in Visualizing Candidate Performance

The conceptual framework should provide a useful way of visualizing the elements of candidate performance.

Content knowledge
Pedagogical content knowledge, skills, dispositions
Professional and pedagogical knowledge, skills, dispositions
Effect on student learning
Assessment/Evaluation System

These knowledge, skills, etc. are transmitted through general education, content & professional studies, and supervised clinical practice under expert guidance. However, curricular delivery must be for some aim or end to avoid just simply standardizing candidates. So the unit's aim in its conceptual framework becomes very critical at this juncture in order to help the unit live its conceptual framework.

For example, suppose a unit identified the following aim: *to facilitate education and growth through empowerment, interconnectedness and change* (Dottin, 2001). That aim should then become the lens through which candidate performance is conceptualized and visualized. If the NCATE Standards then outline the evidence of candidate performance as coming from content knowledge, pedagogical content knowledge, skills, and dispositions, professional and pedagogical knowledge, skills and dispositions, and the candidate's impact on P-12 learning, then the unit might conceptualize its operation accordingly.

Unit Aim: To facilitate education and growth through individual empowerment, interconnectedness, and change.

Candidate Knowledge would then be a form of empowerment since according to the unit's conceptual framework acquiring knowledge, skills, and dispositions is the vehicle to enable candidates to exercise control over their professional practice.

Unit Aim: To facilitate education and growth through individual empowerment, interconnectedness, and change.

Candidates may be seen as a community of learners and thus reinforce interconnectedness since according to the unit's conceptual framework having candidates recognize their common needs and aspirations, and being able to relate to their learners in supportive ways (e.g., technologically), and be able to celebrate and value diversity

---

> Unit Aim: To facilitate education and growth through individual empowerment, interconnectedness, and change.
>
> **The Assessment and Evaluation System may be seen as a catalyst for change** since the unit's conceptual framework would have stated the importance of providing candidates with the orientation, awareness, and commitment to improving their professional practice and P-12 learning.

In living the conceptual framework in a manner above, the unit would then be able to move from its aim through the NCATE Standards requirements in standards 1, 2, 3, and 4 to manifest the candidate performance learning outcomes delineated in the conceptual framework.

The same conceptualization may be applied to faculty performance and to the elements of faculty performance as outlined in the NCATE Standards:

Qualifications

Teaching

Scholarship of the classroom

Service

Collaboration

Evaluation

Professional development.

Living the Conceptual Framework in Visualizing Faculty Performance

> Unit Aim: To facilitate education and growth through individual empowerment, interconnectedness, and change.
>
> **Faculty function as teaching would then be a form of empowerment** since according to the unit's conceptual framework faculty sharing their knowledge, skills, and dispositions with candidates would be done in ways that enable candidates to experience their own competence, creativity, and potential and consequently, exercise control over their professional lives in the classroom or other school personnel roles.

Unit Aim: To facilitate education and growth through individual empowerment, interconnectedness, and change.

Faculty function through research and creative activity would then be a form of change since according to the unit's conceptual framework faculty's commitment to the importance of scholarly and rigorous research would not be externally driven, but instead would be derived from the internal push to discover and understand the variables and forces that either facilitate or impede the learning process and, consequently, would be disposed to the improvement of the human condition.

Unit Aim: To facilitate education and growth through individual empowerment, interconnectedness, and change.

Faculty function through service would then be a form of interconnectedness since according to the unit's conceptual framework faculty should relate to others in helpful and supportive ways and be active participants in the process of shaping and developing public policy in the areas of education and human welfare.

In living the conceptual framework in a manner above, the unit would then be able to move from its aim through the NCATE Standards requirements in standards 1, 2, 3, and 4 to manifest faculty performance as community action to achieve the unit's vision.

Living the Conceptual Framework in Visualizing Unit Leadership Performance

The same conceptualization may also be applied to unit governance performance and to the elements of unit leadership performance as outlined in the NCATE Standards: Leadership – to enhance strategic planning and continuous improvement, budget, personnel – workload policies and the means for the improvement of facilities, and resources including technology.

Unit Aim: To facilitate education and growth through individual empowerment, interconnectedness, and change.

Unit leadership would induce empowerment by helping all unit personnel to be effective professionals. Unit leadership in this context would use the tools of administration to assist personnel to acquire the knowledge, skills, and dispositions necessary to exercise control over their organizational lives.

Unit Aim: To facilitate education and growth through individual empowerment, interconnectedness, and change.

Unit leadership would foster interconnectedness by enhancing the interconnectedness of all those individuals having a vital interest in the unit. This interconnectedness would form the basis of the unit's professional community; a community predicated upon the notion that all educational stakeholders in a professional community should relate to each other in helpful and supportive ways whatever their differences. In this context, the unit's professional community would go beyond the university's campus and would include all groups that have a vital interest in helping the unit prepare teachers and other school personnel. Unit leadership would work to foster interconnectedness through the unit's governance system by communication among and between members of the community, by moving the community to action, and by getting the community to work toward the unit's aim and vision.

Unit Aim: To facilitate education and growth through individual empowerment, interconnectedness, and change.

Unit leadership would facilitate change through organizational renewal. This means that unit leadership would use an administrative process to help elucidate the unit's vision, mission, aim, and outcomes; to secure necessary resources for achieving the unit's aim and outcomes; to help unit personnel solve problems and overcome barriers; and to help unit faculty and staff achieve their goals.

By using its educational aim to in its conceptual framework to visualize and conceptualize the NCATE Standards the unit would be framing the kind of environment conducive to helping the unit live the kind of moral life it has articulated for its community.

NCATE Standards Requisites: Living the Conceptual Framework through Indicators of Evidence

An NCATE Unit Accreditation Board policy promulgated in 2002 encouraged institutions to address, in Part II of their Institutional Report(s), the structural elements of their conceptual framework(s): "In describing the conceptual framework in their IR, institutions are encouraged to provide an overview of the framework by addressing the Structural Elements of the Conceptual Framework, as outlined on page 12 of the NCATE standards manual (2002)." This policy helps Board of Examiners teams to first understand how the unit lays out its conceptual framework with respect to the requisite structural elements.

On the other hand, according to the NCATE Standards (2002), Board of Examiners teams must also look for evidence of the conceptual framework throughout the standards (to see how the unit is living its conceptual framework). This means that a unit should be able to lay out the Standards in a manner that would enable any visitor to easily see how the unit is living its conceptual framework in a manner that is consistent with standards requisites. The vehicle by which the foregoing is shared is, of course, the unit's **Institutional Report**.

The indicators of evidence (i.e., the expectations) vis-à-vis the unit living its conceptual framework through the NCATE Standards (2002) are:

> Shared Vision: The unit's conceptual framework(s) describes the vision and purpose of a unit's efforts in preparing educators to work in P-12 schools....
>
> Coherence: The unit's conceptual framework(s) provides a system for ensuring coherence among curriculum, instruction, field experiences, clinical practice, and assessment across a candidate's program.
>
> Professional Commitments and Dispositions: The unit's conceptual(s) framework clearly articulates its professional commitments to knowledge, teaching competence, and student learning. It has outlined the dispositions that the faculty value in teachers and other professional school personnel.
>
> Commitment to Diversity: The unit's conceptual framework(s) reflects the unit's commitment to preparing candidates to support learning for all students and provides a conceptual understanding of how knowledge, dispositions, and skills related to diversity are integrated across the curriculum, instruction, field experiences, clinical practice, assessments, and evaluation.
>
> Commitment to Technology: The unit's conceptual framework(s) reflects the unit's commitment to preparing candidates who are able to use educational technology to help all students learn; it also provides a conceptual understanding of how knowledge, dispositions, and skills related to educational and information technology are integrated across the curriculum, instruction, field experiences, clinical practice, assessments, and evaluation.
>
> Candidate Proficiencies Aligned with Professional and State Standards: The unit's conceptual framework(s) provides the context for developing and assessing candidate proficiencies based on professional, state, and institutional standards (p. 13).

So to demonstrate evidence of its living its conceptual framework, a unit should:

a. Address the structural elements of a conceptual framework as outlined on page 12 of the NCATE Standards (2002) - Vision, Mission, Philosophy, Aim/purposes, Outcomes/goals, Knowledge Bases, Candidate Proficiencies, Alignment with Standards, and Assessment System. .

b. Address the indicators of evidence as outlined on page 13 of the NCATE Standards (2002) – Shared Vision, Coherence, Professional Commitments and Dispositions, and Alignment with Professional and State Standards.

c. Articulate how the unit is living its conceptual framework as it responds to the 6 NCATE Unit Standards – Candidate Knowledge, Skills, and Dispositions, Assessment System and Unit Evaluation, Field Experiences and Clinical Practice, Diversity, Faculty Qualifications, Performance, and Development, and Unit Governance and Resources. .

The foregoing may be captured accordingly:

Institutional Report	Institutional Report
Part 1	Part 2
Describe Structural Elements	Use 6 NCATE Standards to provide evidence that Unit is Living its Conceptual Framework
** Show link between Structural Elements and Indicators of Evidence - how vision/mission is shared - the connection between purposes and learning experiences - what the unit is prepared to do with regard to candidate learning and its impact on student learning - commitments to particular knowledge, skills, and dispositions including diversity and technology - the context for developing and assessing candidate proficiencies based on institutional, state and professional standards.	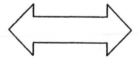

Correspondingly, the Board of Examiners Report should also in its Part 1 describe the structural elements of a unit's conceptual framework, and the link between the structural elements and the indicators of evidence, and in Part II describe how the unit uses the conceptual framework to help it meet the NCATE Standards.

To show the link between the structural elements of the unit's conceptual framework and the "indicators of evidence," warrants attention to the NCATE 6 Standards. For example, a unit may clearly articulate its vision on paper. However, that vision only becomes operational when it is shared. With whom it is shared and to seek what ends in its use should be a manifestation of the unit's intent to live its conceptual framework, and concurrently meet NCATE Professional Standards in so doing.

This may be done by taking the "indicators of evidence" and looking carefully at the 6 NCATE Standards for explicit or implicit language of the indicators (see table below)

	Shared Vision	Coherence	Learning K-S-D	Diversity K-S-D	Technology K-S-D	Align with stds
Std. 1			I	I	I	I
Std. 2		D	D	D	D	D
Std. 3	D	D	D	D	D	D
Std. 4		I	I	I	I	I
Std. 5	D	D	D	D	D	
Std. 6	I	I	I	I	I	I

K-S-D=candidate learning proficiencies
D=direct connections in standard elements [reference to conceptual framework] to indicator of evidence
I=indirect connections in standard elements [reference to conceptual framework] to indicator of evidence

To live the conceptual framework requires that a unit understands that it is not living the abstract term "conceptual framework." Instead, a unit is living the structural elements of its conceptual framework as operationalized in the unit's effort to meet the 6 NCATE Standards. Consequently, the reference to the term "conceptual framework" in the respective standards must be translated according to the appropriate structural element of a conceptual framework and the related indicator of evidence of that structural element (see table below).

STRUCTURAL ELEMENTS (of conceptual framework)	EVALUATIVE CRITERIA (Evidence of the conceptual framework(s) throughout the standards)
- Vision/Mission - Philosophy, purposes, Aim - Goals/outcomes, knowledge base(s), candidate proficiencies - Candidate proficiencies and alignment with standards - System for assessment	- Is vision/mission shared? (shared vision) - What is the connection between philosophy, learning outcomes, curricular experiences? (coherence) - What is the unit prepared to do regarding candidate learning including commitments to diversity and technology? (professional commitments and dispositions including commitments to diversity and technology) - What is the context for developing and assessing proficiencies? (candidate proficiencies aligned with professional and state standards)

Operationalizing Structural Elements and Indicators of Evidence of Conceptual Framework

Living Conceptual Framework through Like-mindedness for Common Ends: Is the unit vision shared?

There is a direct connection in two of the elements of Standard 3 to the unit sharing its vision. The element of COLLABORATION BETWEEN UNIT AND SCHOOL PARTNERS highlights the need for collaboration between unit and school partners in designing, implementing, and evaluating the unit's conceptual framework(s) and the school program. The reference to the term "conceptual framework" here may logically refer to the unit's vision and the indicator of evidence vis-à-vis shared vision. Collaboration provides the unit the opportunity to share many aspects of its conceptual framework. In this instance, the aspect of "vision" takes the spotlight.

The element of DESIGN, IMPLEMENTATION, and AND EVALUATION OF FIELD EXPERIENCES AND CLINICAL PRACTICE suggests that both field experiences and clinical practice extend the unit's conceptual framework(s) into practice through well designed opportunities to learn though doing. Here again, the logical connection is to extending the unit's shared vision in order to achieve common ends.

There is also a direct connection in three elements of Standard 5 to the unit sharing its vision. In the element MODELING BEST PROFESSIONAL PRACTICES IN TEACHING the standard requirement is that teaching by the professional faculty reflects the unit's conceptual framework(s)... It would seem quite logical here that faculty teaching is guided by the shared vision of the unit. The element of COLLABORATION expects that faculty are actively engaged as a community of learners regarding the conceptual framework(s) and scholarship of the classroom. Since there is no community without a common end, then the focus of the community in this context should be on extending the unit's vision in the classroom. The element of UNIT FACILITATION OF PROFESSIONAL DEVELOPMENT states that based upon needs identified in faculty evaluations, the unit provides opportunities for faculty to develop new knowledge and skills, especially as they relate to the conceptual framework(s) ....In other words, faculty professional development should be guided by the unit's shared vision. In Standard 6, the element UNIT LEADERSHIP AND AUTHORITY while not having a direct reference to the term conceptual framework, implicitly assumes that the leadership of the unit would use the unit's vision to deliver and operate coherent programs of study.

Living Conceptual Framework by Enhancing Coherence: The Visible Connection between Purposes and Learning Experiences

Making connections between unit purpose and learning experiences automatically brings to the fore the connection between philosophy, curriculum, and assessment of learning. Consequently, there is a direct connection in the Standard 2 element of ASSESSMENT SYSTEM.

The expectation in the standard that the unit has developed an assessment system with its professional community that reflects the conceptual framework(s) ... may only be manifested if there links between and among the unit's philosophy in the conceptual framework, the curriculum to operationalize that philosophy, and the instruction, learning experiences, and evaluations ("evaluations must be purposeful, evolving from the unit's conceptual framework(s) and program goals." – Supporting Explanation, NCATE Standards, 2002, p. 23).

The call for coherence is also manifested in the Standard 3 element, COLLABORATION BETWEEN UNIT AND SCHOOL PARTNERS. The reference in this element to the term conceptual framework clearly points to the kind of collaboration between unit and school partners in which both sides work to make connections between expressed unit purpose in its conceptual framework, and the kinds of learning experiences in field and clinical practice that would support the expressed purpose.

Coherence is also expressed in the Standard 3 element, DESIGN, IMPLEMENTATION, and AND EVALUATION OF FIELD EXPERIENCES AND CLINICAL PRACTICE. The call in the element for field and clinical practice to reflect the conceptual framework is clearly a call for connecting purpose in the conceptual framework and learning in the field vis-à-vis experiences and assessment instruments.

There is also a call for the unit to connect its philosophy of education to the curricular experiences provided that enhances the concept of diversity. While there is no explicit language in Standard 4 with regard to the term conceptual framework, the implication is clear in the Standard 4 element, DESIGN, IMPLEMENTATION, AND EVALUATION OF CURRICULUM AND EXPERIENCES that the unit must have particular beliefs about the idea of "diversity," (the vision and philosophy of the unit) that might shape how the unit "... articulates the proficiencies (learning outcomes) that candidates are expected to develop during their professional program. Curriculum and accompanying field experiences are designed to help candidates understand the importance of diversity in teaching and learning.... [Candidates] demonstrate dispositions that value fairness and learning by all students" (NCATE Standards, 2002, p. 29).

There are several elements in Standard 5 that address the need for coherence and the use of the unit's conceptual framework in operationalizing that coherence.

The element, MODELING BEST PROFESSIONAL PRACTICES IN TEACHING shows the visible connection between the vision, purposes and aim, learning outcomes and assessments in the unit's conceptual framework and teaching in the unit. The element, COLLABORATION shows the visible connection between the vision, philosophy and aim, learning outcomes and assessments in the unit's conceptual framework, and faculty being actively engaged as a community of learners working to improve teaching, learning, and their scholarship of the classroom. In addition, the element, UNIT FACILITATION OF PROFESSIONAL DEVELOPMENT shows the visible connection between the vision and philosophy, learning outcomes, and assessments in the unit's conceptual framework, and faculty opportunities for professional development: "Based upon the needs identified in faculty evaluations, the unit provides opportunities for faculty to develop new knowledge and skills, especially as they relate to the conceptual framework, ..." (NCATE Standards, 2002, p. 36).

Finally, in the Standard 6 element, UNIT LEADERSHIP AND AUTHORITY there is an implicit connection to coherence in the call for the unit leadership "... to plan, deliver, and operate coherent programs of study" (NCATE Standards, 2002, p. 38). It would seem that the foregoing can only be effective if the leadership is operating from a vision, a philosophy, and agreed upon learning outcomes and assessments, all of which are elements of the unit's conceptual framework.

Living Conceptual Framework through Professional Commitments and Dispositions: The Visible Expression of What the Unit is Prepared To Do Regarding Candidate Learning and its Effect on Student Learning

All elements in Standard 1 (except the two on STUDENT LEARNING FOR TEACHER CANDIDATES, and STUDENT LEARNING FOR OTHER SCHOOL PERSONNEL) call for connections between the learning outcomes and candidate proficiencies articulated in the unit's conceptual framework, and the knowledge, skills and disposition delineated in state and professional standards.

The unit, therefore, lives its conceptual framework (even though there is no explicit use of the word conceptual framework in Standard 1 and its elements) as candidates demonstrate the learning outcomes and proficiencies in the conceptual framework and that are aligned with state, and professional standards. The foregoing is, however, reinforced in the Supporting Explanation of Standard 1:

> ... candidates preparing to teach or work as other professional educators in P-12 schools are expected to demonstrate the learning proficiencies identified in the unit's conceptual framework(s), which should be aligned with standards for P-12 students, the standards of national professional organizations, and state licensing standards.
> ... The unit articulates candidate dispositions as part of its conceptual framework(s) (NCATE Standards, 2002, p. 17, p. 19).

It is these candidate proficiencies in the unit's conceptual framework that, therefore, enable the candidate to affect P-12 student learning.

Reflecting the unit's conceptual framework as noted in Standard 2's element, ASSESSMENT SYSTEM logically extends to the incorporation of the candidate proficiencies in the unit's assessment system (institutional standards) that are aligned with state and professional standards . In addition, the Standard 2 elements, DATA COLLECTION, ANALYSIS, AND EVALUATION, and USE OF DATA FOR PROGRAM IMPROVEMENT tacitly expect that that data gathered on the candidates' acquisition and demonstration of the proficiencies that are aligned with state and professional standards (including effect on P-12 student learning) will be used for continuous improvement of the unit and its community.

What the unit is prepared to do regarding candidate learning and its effect on P-12 student learning emerges in Standard 3 and the element, COLLABORATION BETWEEN UNIT AND SCHOOL PARTNERS. The clear expectation is that school-based faculty, as part of the unit's professional community, would assist the unit in implementing and evaluating candidate proficiencies (the knowledge, skills, and dispositions delineated in the unit's conceptual framework) in field and clinical practice. To do so, of course, requires collaboration between the unit and school-based faculty.

In addition, the Standard 3 element, DESIGN, IMPLEMENTATION, AND EVALUATION OF FIELD EXPERIENCES AND CLINICAL PRACTICE assumes that what the unit is prepared to do vis-à-vis candidate learning and its effect on P-12 student learning is demonstrated in both field experiences and clinical practice as these experiences and practice assist candidates to further develop and refine "... the content, professional, and pedagogical knowledge, skills, and dispositions delineated in standards" (NCATE Standards, 2002, p. 26).

Standard 4 also affords the unit an opportunity to demonstrate what it is prepared to do with regard to candidate learning and its effect on P-12 student learning. The standard element, DESIGN, IMPLENENTATION, AND EVALUATION OF CURRICULUM AND EXPERIENCES while not making any explicit reference to the word "conceptual framework" implicitly assumes the knowledge, skills, and dispositions (that is, candidate proficiencies) in the conceptual framework and related to diversity (including proficiencies for working with students with exceptionalities) would be developed during exposure to the program's curriculum, and practiced during field experiences and clinical practice. Since, according to Dewey (1916/1944) we never teach directly but by means of the environment, then the Standard 4 elements of EXPERIENCES WORKING WITH DIVERSE FACULTY, EXPERIENCES WORKING WITH DIVERSE CANDIDATES, AND EXPERIENCES WORKING WITH DIVERSE STUDENTS IN P-12 SCHOOLS contribute to helping candidates understand the importance of diversity in teaching and learning.

Standard 5 affords several opportunities for the unit to show what it is prepared to do regarding candidate learning and its effect on P-12 student learning. The element, MODELING BEST PROFESSIONAL PRACTICES IN TEACHING notes that "Teaching by the professional education faculty reflects the unit's conceptual framework(s) ..." (NCATE Standards, 2002, p. 34). Naturally that reflection is really the faculty's commitment to helping candidates acquire the proficiencies delineated in the unit's conceptual framework through its teaching. The element, COLLABORATION calls for faculty to be "... actively engaged as a community of learners regarding the conceptual framework(s) and scholarship of the classroom" (NCATE Standards, 2002, p. 35). A community of learners is focused on learning, and as such, must attend to what the unit is prepared to do with regard to learning, i.e., the knowledge, skills, and dispositions in the unit's conceptual framework.

In addition, the element, UNIT FACILITATION OF PROFESSIONAL DEVELOPMENT calls for opportunities for faculty development that is linked to what the unit is prepared to do regarding candidate learning (i.e., the knowledge, skills, and dispositions in the conceptual framework).

The element in Standard 6, UNIT LEADERSHIP AND AUTHORITY, implicitly expresses what the unit is prepared to do with regard to candidate learning and its effect on P-12 student learning by requiring that "The unit effectively manages or coordinates all programs so that their candidates are prepared to meet standards" (NCATE Standards, 2002, p. 38). The logical expectation here is that the unit leadership would manage and coordinate all programs so that they stay true to the professional commitments and dispositions outlined in the conceptual framework.

Living Conceptual Framework through Aligning Candidate Proficiencies with State and Professional Standards: The Context for Developing and Assessing Candidate Proficiencies

Finally, there should be a context for developing and assessing candidate proficiencies. According to the National Commission on Teaching and America's Future (1996) "Standards for teaching are the linchpin for transforming current systems of preparation, licensing, certification, and on-going development so that they better support student learning" (67). The commission goes on to suggest:

> Clearly, if students are to achieve high standards, we can expect no less from their teachers and other educators. The first priority is reaching agreement on what teachers should know and be able to do in order to help students succeed. Unaddressed for decades, this task has recently been completed by three professional bodies, The National Council for Accreditation of Teacher Education (NCATE), the Interstate New Teachers Assessment and Support Consortium (INTASC), and the National Board for Professional Teaching Standards (The National Board). Their combined efforts to set standards for teacher education, beginning teacher licensing, and advanced certification outline a continuum of teacher development throughout the career. These standards offer the most powerful tools we have for reaching and rejuvenating the soul of the profession (Summary Report, What Matters Most: Teaching for America's Future, September 1996, 18).

The development of professional accountability in teacher education may therefore be seen as a continuum that links a College of Education (a unit) responsible for the initial preparation of candidates, to the public authority for its operation, a State, to the induction process for candidates into the field (school sites), to the professional and learned societies that shape what is taken for knowledge in the respective fields (national societies), to the accomplished professional as judged by the National Board for Professional Teaching Standards (NBPTS). The foregoing may be captured accordingly:

	STATE/PUBLIC (Money, management, control accountability)	
INITIAL PREPARATION (Unit) (National Council for Accreditation of Teacher Education)	INDUCTION (Candidate induction) (Interstate New Teachers Assessment and Support Consortium)	PROFESSIONAL PRACTICE (National Board for Professional Teaching Standards)
	SPECIALIZED PROFESSIONAL ASSOCIATIONS (Professional accountability)	

Quality assurance in teacher education when viewed through a three-legged stool metaphor (NCATE, INTASC, NBPTS), enables Schools/Colleges of Education to be guided by institutional, state, and professional standards, especially if standards are defined in a normative sense as measures of what ought to be. The pursuit to align standards is, therefore, a pursuit to improve the preparation of teachers and other school personnel through standards-based reform. The goal of the reform is enhanced student learning in P-12 settings.

A school/college seeking national accreditation is, therefore, required to lay out its conceptual framework in a manner that "provides a context for aligning professional and state standards with candidate proficiencies expected by the unit and programs for the preparation of educators" (NCATE 2000 Unit Standards, March 31, 2000, 2).

The context for professional development is manifested first in Standard 1.

The elements, CONTENT KNOWLEDGE FOR TEACHER CANDIDATES, CONTENT KNOWLEDGE FOR OTHER SCHOOL PERSONNEL, PEDAGOGICAL CONTENT KNOWLEDGE FOR TEACHER CANDIDATES, PROFESSIONAL AND PEDAGOGICAL KNOWLEDGE AND SKILLS FOR TEACHER CANDIDATES, PROFESSIONAL KNOWLEDGE AND SKILLS FOR OTHER SCHOOL PERSONNEL, and DISPOSITIONS FOR ALL CANDIDATES all call for an alignment between the candidate proficiencies (institutional standards) in the unit's conceptual framework, and state and professional standards.

The context for developing and assessing candidate proficiencies is also manifested in Standard 2. The element, ASSESSMENT SYSTEM notes that "The unit, with the involvement of its professional community, is implementing an assessment system that reflects the conceptual framework(s) and incorporates candidate proficiencies outlined in professional and state standards" (NCATE Standards, 2002, p. 21). In addition, the element, USE OF DATA FOR PROGRAM IMPROVEMENT logically expects that the unit will ensure quality in its institutional standards through alignment with and use of state and professional standards (the new NCATE Program Review process started in 2004 exemplifies this quality assurance connection).

The context for developing and assessing candidate proficiencies is also framed in Standards 3, 4 and 6. The elements in Standard 3 of COLLABORATION BETWEEN UNIT AND SCHOOL PARTNERS and DESIGN, IMPLEMENTATION, AND EVALUATION OF FIELD EXPERIENCES AND CLINICAL PRACTICE harbor an expectation that unit and school partners would work to ensure that candidate knowledge, skills, and dispositions for field/clinical practice (institutional standards) are consistent with state and professional standards. The element in Standard 4, DESIGN, IMPLEMENTATION, AND EVALUATION OF CURRICULUM AND EXPERIENCES calls for the proficiencies for working with students from diverse backgrounds and with exceptionalities, as outlined in the institutional standards in the unit's conceptual framework, to be linked to state and professional standards, while the element in Standard 6, UNIT LEADERSHIP AND AUTHORITY has an expectation that the unit leadership will coordinate all programs to meet institutional, state and professional standards.

Showing Evidence of Living the Conceptual Framework through the Institutional Report (IR)

The NCATE *Handbook for Accreditation Visits* (2002) notes the following:

> The professional education unit is required to write and submit an institutional report (IR) that describes the unit's conceptual framework and evidence that demonstrates that the six standards are met. In continuing accreditation visits, the IR also serves as primary documentation of the unit's growth and development since the last accreditation visit (p. 45).

The *Handbook* (2002) also states:

> The discussion of the framework(s) should concisely summarize the six structural elements of the conceptual framework and each of the six expectations listed as *Evidence for Conceptual Framework(s)* in the NCATE Unit Standards document: (1) shared vision, (2) coherence, (3) professional commitments and dispositions, (4) commitment to diversity, (5) commitment to technology, and (6) candidate proficiencies aligned with professional and state standards (pp. 47-48).

So, how might the unit live its conceptual framework through its Institutional Report? First, the unit must realize that it is really living the structural elements of its conceptual framework. It must first have a desired future, a vision, before it can address how that vision is being shared. The evaluative criteria by which the unit can determine the extent to which it is living the structural elements of its conceptual framework are thus laid out in the NCATE Standards (2002) as "Evidence of the Conceptual Framework(s) throughout the Standards" that is "Shared Vision... Coherence ... Professional Commitments and Dispositions... Commitment to Diversity... Commitment to Technology... Candidate Proficiencies Aligned with Professional and State Standards" (p. 13).

Part II of the IR should therefore address the structural elements of the unit's conceptual framework (vision, mission, philosophy, aim, outcomes, candidate proficiencies, alignment with standards, and assessment system), and provide an introductory link to how the unit will provide evidence later in the IR (Part III) of living those structural elements of its framework through the NCATE suggested evaluative criteria and according the standards requirements in the six standards.

Institutions going through first time accreditation would have submitted its entire conceptual framework as part of the NCATE preconditions requirement. Consequently, a concise summary of the structural elements in Part II of the IR would be appropriate for first time institutions. On the other hand, institutions going through a continuing accreditation visit should attend to the strengths of the elements in Part II of their IR's, and to relevant changes made to and evaluations of any of the elements since the last visit.

Once Part II regarding the conceptual framework is completed then the unit must direct its attention to providing evidence of how it is living its conceptual framework through the six NCATE Standards. A useful means to that end is for the unit to take each of the six standards, identify in each standard explicit or implicit reference to the word "conceptual framework" and articulate the evidence called for and that must be presented to a Board of Examiners team.

Evidence of Conceptual Framework in Standard 1	
Evidence in Standard	Providing evidence in IR
[Supporting Explanation] "Candidates ... demonstrate the learning proficiencies identified in the unit's conceptual framework(s), ... aligned with standards for P-12 students, the standards Of national professional Organizations, and state Licensing standards" (p. 17) "The unit articulates candidate Dispositions as part of its Conceptual framework(s)" (p. 19).	Clearly identify the following proficiencies: Content Content for Other School Personnel Pedagogical Content Professional and Pedagogical knowledge and skills Professional knowledge and skills for Other School Personnel Dispositions

Evidence of Conceptual Framework in Standard 2	
Evidence in Standard	Providing evidence in IR
[Rubric] "The unit with the involvement of its professional community, is implementing an assessment system that reflects the conceptual framework(s) and incorporates candidate proficiencies outlined in professional and state standards" (p. 21)	Show how the unit's assessment system reflects the unit's philosophical intentions, actions, and beliefs. Show how the unit's assessment system is linked to the learning commitments (candidate proficiencies) including proficiencies related to diversity and technology, and how these are aligned with state and professional standards.
[Supporting Explanation] "Evaluations must be Purposeful, evolving from the Unit's conceptual framework(s) and program goals" (p. 23).	Show that unit operations are evaluated in a manner consistent with the beliefs, aim, outcomes, and assessments in the conceptual framework.

Evaluation must apprise the behavior of candidates since it is change in these behaviors which is sought in education. Evaluation must involve more than a single appraisal at any one time since to see whether change has taken place it is necessary to make an appraisal at an early point and other appraisals at later points to identify changes that may be occurring. On this basis one is not able to evaluate an instructional program by testing students at the end of the program. In order to have some estimate of the permanence of the learning it is necessary to have still another point of evaluation which is made sometimes after the instruction has been completed.

Hence, schools and colleges are conducting follow-up studies of their graduates in order to get further evidence as to the permanence or impermanence of the learning which may have been acquired during the time the candidates were in the program.

Evidence of Conceptual Framework in Standard 3

Evidence in Standard	Providing evidence in IR
[Rubric] "Both unit and school-based faculty are involved in designing, implementing, and evaluating the unit's conceptual framework(s) and the school program; ..." (p. 25) "Both field experiences and clinical practice reflect the unit's conceptual framework(s) and help candidates continue to develop the content, professional, and pedagogical knowledge, skills, and dispositions delineated in standards" (p. 26)	Show how the unit and school-based faculty are involved in designing the unit's desired future; the unit's philosophy, and beliefs system. Show how the unit and school-based faculty are implementing the learning outcomes and assessment system. Show how the unit and school-based faculty are involved in the alignment of standards and in judging candidate effectiveness.

Evidence of Conceptual Framework in Standard 4

Evidence in Standard	Providing evidence in IR
[Implicit in Standard and Rubric] "The unit designs, implements, and evaluates curriculum and experiences for candidates to acquire and apply the knowledge, skills, and dispositions necessary to help all students learn" (p. 29). "The unit clearly articulates the proficiencies that candidates are expected to develop during their professional program" (p. 29).	Show the philosophical value commitments to diversity. Show the commitments to diversity in the learning outcomes. Show the commitments to diversity in the alignment of standards. Show the commitments to assessing diversity.

Evidence of Conceptual Framework in Standard 5	
Evidence in Standard	Providing evidence in IR
[Rubric] "Teaching by the professional Education faculty reflects the unit's Conceptual framework(s) ..." (p. 34). "Faculty are actively engaged as a community of learners regarding the conceptual framework(s) and scholarship of the classroom" (p. 35). "Based upon needs identified in faculty evaluations, the unit provides opportunities for faculty to develop new knowledge and skills, especially as they relate to the conceptual framework(s)..." (p. 36).	Show the unit faculty's collaboration with colleagues regarding the unit's desired future, and its philosophy. Show how teaching reflects the unit's vision and philosophy. Show how teaching is helping candidates acquire the learning outcomes. Show the unit's on-going effort to improve and translate its desired future, and philosophical beliefs, and how success is determined through unit unit outcomes and assessments.

Evidence of Conceptual Framework in Standard 6	
Evidence in Standard	Providing evidence in IR
[Implicit in Standard and Rubric] "The unit has the leadership, authority, ... for the preparation of candidates to meet professional, state, and institutional standards" (p. 38). "The unit has the leadership and authority to plan, deliver, and operate coherent programs of study" (p. 38).	Show how the unit's leadership is manifesting the unit's vision and mission. Show how coherent planning and delivery of programs are based on the unit's philosophy Show the unit leadership's commitment to learning outcomes.

Living the Conceptual Framework: Facilitating Unit Renewal through Short and Long-Term Goals

To begin the process of goals development a unit may be guided by John Dewey's dictum that "... aims relate always to results" (Dewey, 1944, 101). However, as Dewey so cogently illuminated the distinction between results and ends is that results follow any "exhibition of energy" while end "possess intrinsic continuity" (Dewey, 1944, 101):

Continuous performance improvement is therefore facilitated by the conceptual framework as the aim of the unit is facilitated by a process of continuous improvement that moves from a conceptual big picture to parts and back to the whole to the use of results to effect change.

To improve presupposes a state in which one is becoming. Having some sense of direction for the development and refinement of improvement goals, strategies and measures, enhances one having some degree of coherence. Continuous improvement should therefore be a matter of assessing oneself against standards of what ought to be and developing a needs index for growth.

Continuous improvement should facilitate the unit's way of making meaning of its decision making in how it delivers its curriculum, how it attends to its candidates, how it enhances faculty vitality, and how unit accountability is provided. In this context, the unit's goals planning is given meaning vis-à-vis what is delivered in order to achieve its aim. This goal focused model leads to a relationship between the unit, its departments and programs, and the products and goals each develops in order to enhance a unified and coherent operation.

Short and long-term goals thus become an extension of the unit's aim, and are not adopted from someone else's goals. These goals will, therefore, reflect the unit's values and sense of purpose. As a result, goals development in the unit should foster on-going unit accountability and performance benchmarks that enhance unit progress and growth.

Goals enhance unit effectiveness by reinforcing the end in the conceptual framework of like-mindedness vis-à-vis pursuing the unit's vision. By connecting its conceptual framework to long term goals, a unit gives further credence to living its conceptual framework. By so doing, a unit is stimulating continued growth in the unit, and looking to improve life lived in common so that the unit's future will be better than its present.

To live its conceptual framework through its goals process, and thereby reinforce the moral dispositions delineated in the conceptual framework, a unit should use the NCATE Standards for the profession as external conditions of what ought to be in terms of candidate performance, field experiences and clinical practice, commitments to diversity and the use of technology, faculty vitality, and unit will and capacity, and then examine its current internal conditions vis-à-vis those areas and identify long- and short-term goals, the achievement of which will facilitate change in the unit's conceptual framework. This process of moving from what ought to be to what is creates a needs index or goals to be achieved. To be effective, this goals process should:

1. Conduct an analysis of external conditions (that is, normative professional expectations built into the NCATE Standards, the standards of the regional accrediting body for the unit, and state standards).
2. Identify a set of unit long-range goals that are compatible with the unit's aim.
3. Identify the unit's programs and department's current operational realities and the short-term goals needed to correct discrepancies between and among professional external expectations and current operational realities.
4. Articulate the steps to achieve the goals (objectives, activities, measures of success, performance criteria).
5. Identify individuals and/or groups responsible for initiating and sustaining the steps toward achieving the short-term goals.
6. Identify timelines for the goals activities and budget necessities.
7. Identify criteria to be used in evaluating progress toward the short-term goals.
8. Identify the governance group(s) responsible for using the results of the short-term goals activity to effect unit and program changes and improvements.

Examples of the above process for the long-term goals (a) to enhance the performance of all candidates, (b) to enhance faculty performance as a means to enhance candidate performance, and (c) to provide the necessary leadership to facilitate the enhancement of both faculty and candidates' performance are below:

Long-term Goal: To enhance the performance of all candidates.
Short-term goal: Enhance curriculum delivery, candidate performance and unit assessment and evaluation systems.
Objectives/activities:
a. increases the use of technology in all programs.
b. develops and implements outcomes for all programs.
c. improves the monitoring and assessing of candidate progress.
d. engages in ongoing systematic evaluation to determine how well the unit is achieving its outcomes.
e. institute processes and procedures for entry into the unit and its programs.
f. provides candidates with an integrated sequence of field and clinical experiences.
g. enhances and expands experiences in diversity.
h. increase intra- and inter-unit collaboration.
i. enhances articulation between the unit and its contiguous community colleges.
j. increase collaboration with P-12 school faculty.

Long-term Goal: To enhance faculty performance as a means to enhance candidates' performance.
Short-term goal: Enhance faculty professional development.
Objectives/activities:
a. increase computer technological support for faculty teaching, research and service.
b. enhances faculty professional development and growth.
c. increase faculty scholarship achievement.
d. increase faculty involvement in the world of practice.

Long-term Goal: To provide the necessary leadership to facilitate the enhancement of both faculty and candidates performance.
Short-term Goal: Enhance unit accountability.
Objectives/activities:
a. facilitates the coordination of programs through the unit's conceptual framework.
b. enhances the unit's communication and decision-making.
c. enhances facilities and resources to support teaching, research, and service.

CHAPTER FOUR

EVALUATING THE CONCEPTUAL FRAMEWORK

The conceptual framework(s) establishes the shared vision for a unit's efforts in preparing educators to work effectively in P-12 schools. It provides direction for programs, courses, teaching, candidate performance, scholarship, service, and unit accountability. The conceptual framework(s) is knowledge-based, articulated, shared, coherent, and consistent with the unit and/or institutional mission, _and continuously evaluated (NCATE Unit Standards, 2002, p. 10)._

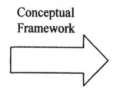

Conceptual Framework	Programs, Courses, Teaching, Candidate Performance, Faculty Performance, Unit Accountability	Assessment System
		Evaluation of Unit Operations

Judging the Worth of the Conceptual Framework

The two points selected by which to measure the worth of a form of social life are the extent in which the interests of a group are shared by all its members, and the fullness and freedom with which it interacts with other groups. An undesirable society, in other words, is one which internally and externally sets up barriers to free intercourse and communication of experience (Dewey, 1916/1944, p. 99).

Dewey's words above might be used as a catalyst for judging the worth of (that is, evaluating) a conceptual framework. For example, if a conceptual framework enhances the interests of the unit being shared by all of its members, then it might be said that the conceptual framework is worthwhile. A unit's conceptual framework may thus be seen as the lens through which persons in the unit view their personal interest in social contexts, and the educative process that enhances the "habits of mind" which are conducive to personal and social transformation.

The act of striving to realize the unit's vision and aim should actually tests the worth of the unit's conceptual framework. According to John Dewey (1916/1944):

> acting upon [an aim] brings to light conditions which had been overlooked. This calls for revision of the original aim; it has to be added to and subtracted from. An aim must, then, be flexible; it must be capable of alteration to meet circumstances" (p. 104).

To evaluate the conceptual framework is to raise the following salient questions: is the conceptual framework improving the life unit members live in common so that the unit's future is better than its past? Is there evidence that the unit's professional community is regulating specific activities in light or in view of the unit's common end?

Acting upon the common end in the conceptual framework should, therefore, bring to light conditions which had been overlooked (in outcomes, candidate proficiencies, assessments, and so on). This calls for revision of the original shared sense of the future and supporting philosophy that make the professional community unique. Just as the unit's professional community would be concerned with the evidence of candidate performance, the community should, in its evaluation of the conceptual framework, ask itself "Are members of the professional community all cognizant of the unit's common end? Are they all interested in the common end? Are there signs of community vis-à-vis the common end? Does each member of the professional community keep others informed as to his/her own purpose and progress vis-à-vis the common end?" Of course, counter evidence to the foregoing would emerge if members of the community used one another to get their own desired results, and if the majority of life experiences in the unit was just giving and taking orders?

So, to evaluate a unit's conceptual framework would require that from time to time, the unit re-examines its decisions and beliefs concerning its outcomes of education by reassessing its arguments and the arguments of others in the light of additional evidence gathered from reading, continued study, and so on, and by reassessing the reasonableness of the moral/ethical theory it holds.

Answering the question as to whether there are better reasons for teaching or for not teaching particular matter to a candidate will require that the unit reconsider its decisions and beliefs concerning the outcomes of teacher education, especially the philosophical and psychological reasons for the outcome.

In other words, a good conceptual framework will create possibilities for a unit to generate working hypotheses to guide the study of and subsequent renewal of its practices and policies. It is the compass for showing how the unit's operation will make life in the unit better for all involved, intellectually, socially, emotionally, **and morally**, and thus creates a professional through mean-ends connection to facilitate the acquisition of moral dispositions.

BIBLIOGRAPHY

Allen, L. (2001, December). From plaques to practice: How schools can breathe life into their guiding beliefs. *Phi Delta Kappan*, 289-293.

"A mindful life" (n.d.). Retrieved, June 21, 2004 from http://www.kathrynpetro.com/mindfullife/archives/000008.html

Barell, J. (1991). *Teaching for thoughtfulness: Classroom strategies to enhance intellectual development.* New York: Longman.

Baron, J. (1985). *Rationality and intelligence.* New York: Cambridge University Press.

Block, P. (1987). *The empowered manager.* San Francisco, CA: Jossey-Bass.

Brown, B. A. & Cocking, R. (Eds.) (1990). *How people learn.* Washington, D.C.: National Academy Press.

Burbules, N. (2004, August/September). Ways of thinking about educational quality. In *Educational Researcher, 33(6),* 4-10.

Costa, A.L. & Kallick, B. (2000). *Habits of mind: Activating & engaging.* Alexandria, VA: Association for Supervision and Curriculum Development.

Costa, A.L. & Garmston, R.J. (1998, spring). Maturing outcomes. *Encounter: Education for Meaning and Social Justice,* 11(1), 10-18.

"Developing a vision, mission and values" (n.d.) Retrieved, June 21, 2004 from http://www.brefigroup.co.uk/facilitation/vision.html

Dewey, J. (1960). *Theory of the moral life.* New York: Holt Rinehart and Winston.

Dewey, J. (1944). *Democracy and education: An introduction to the philosophy of education.* New York: The Free Press.

Dewey, J. & Tufts, J. H. (1913). *Ethics.* New York: Henry Holt and Company.

Dove, R. (1998). Retrieved, June 21, 2004 from http://www.parshift.com/Essays/essay045.htm

Dufour, R. and Eaker, R. (1998). Professional learning communities at work: Best practices for enhancing student achievement. Alexandria, Virginia: Association for Supervision and Curriculum Development.

Fitzgibbons, R. (1981). *Making educational decisions: An introduction to philosophy of education.* New York: Harcourt Brace Jovanovich.

Fullan, M. (1993). *Changing forces: Probing the depths of educational reform.* London: The Falmer Press.

Gardner, H. (1985). *Frames of mind: The theory of multiple intelligences.* New York: Basic Books.

Hansen, D. (2001). *Exploring the moral heart of teaching: Toward a teacher's creed.* New York: Teachers College Press.

"I dream of giving birth to a child who will ask 'mother, what was war'" (n.d.). Brochure. The Lion and Lamb Peace Arts Center, Bluffton College, Bluffton, Ohio.

Iran-Nejad, A. (1995). Constructivism as substitute for memorization in learning: Meaning is created by the learner. *Education,* 116, 16-31.

Ivie, S. D. (2003). *On the wings of metaphor.* San Francisco, CA: Caddo Gap Press.

Jones, L. B. (1996). *The path: Creating your mission statement for work and for life.* New York: Hyperion.

Kardash, C.M. & Sinatra, G.M. (2003). Epistemological beliefs and dispositions: Are we measuring the same construct? Resources in Education. ERIC Document Reproduction Service No. ED 479-164. Washington, D.C.: Clearinghouse on Teacher Education.

Kerka, S. (2003). Appreciative inquiry: Trends and issues alert. Resources in Education. ERIC Document Reproduction Service. No. ED 473-671. Columbus, OH: Clearinghouse on Adult, Career, and Vocational Education.

King, M. (1988, winter). Ordinary Olympians. *In Context,* (18). Sequim, WA: North Olympic Living Lightly Association.

Koppich, J.E. & Knapp, M.S. (1998, April). Federal research investment and the improvement of teaching 1980-1997. Seattle, WA: Center for the Study of Teaching & Policy.

Lipman, M., Sharp, A. M., & Oscanyan, F.S. (1977). *Ethical inquiry: Instructional manual to accompany Lisa.* Upper Montclair, NJ: Institute for the Advancement of Philosophy for Children.

Maki, P. (2002, January-February). Developing an assessment plan to learn about student learning. *Journal of Academic Librarianship,* Vol. 28 (Issues 1-2), pp. 8-13.

National Commission on Teaching and America's Future. (1996). *What matters most: Teaching for America's future.* New York: Author.

National Council for Accreditation of Teacher Education. (2002). *Professional standards for the accreditation of schools, colleges, and departments of education.* Washington, D.C.: NCATE.

North Glade Elementary. (n.d.). Mission/vision. Retrieved July 1, 2004, from http://nges.dadeschools.net/mission%20statement.htm

Norton, D. (1995). *Democracy and moral development.* Berkeley, CA: University of California Press.

Oakeshott, M. (1989). *The voice of liberal learning: Michael Oakeshott on education.* (T. Fuller, Ed.). New Haven, CT: Yale University Press.

Ozmon, H. & Craver, S. (1990). *Philosophical foundations of education.* 4th edition. Columbus, Ohio: Merrill Publishing Company.

Pascale, P. (1990). *Managing on the edge.* New York: Touchstone.

Peterson, M. (1995). Harnessing the power of vision. Ten steps to creating a strategic vision and action plan for your community. Preparing your community for the 21st century series. Resources in Education. ERIC Document Reproduction Service No. ED 383-824.

Piaget, J. (1959). *Judgment and reasoning in the child.* Totowa, NJ: Littlefield, Addams & Company.

Piaget, J. & Inhelder, B. (1970). *The psychology of the child.* New York: Basic Books.

Pratt, D. D. (n.d). Good teaching: one size fits all? In *An update on teaching theory,* Jovita Ross-Gordon (Ed.), San Francisco: Jossey-Bass, Publishers.

Richardson, V. Editor. (2001). *Handbook of research on teaching. 4th Edition.* Washington, D.C.: American Educational Research Association.

Rogers, C. (1982). *Freedom to learn in the eighties.* Columbus, OH: Merrill.

Sa, W., West, R.F., & Stanovich, K.E. (1999). The domain specificity and generality of belief bias in reasoning and judgment. *Journal of Educational Psychology,* 91(3), 497-510.

Senge, P. (1990). *The fifth discipline: The art and practice of the learning organization.* New York: Doubleday Currency.

Sockett, H. (2004). Character, rules, & relationships. A pre-conference workshop presentation at the annual meeting of the American Association of Colleges of Teacher Education, Chicago, Illinois.

Stanovich, K.E. (1999). *Who is rational? Studies of individual differences in reasoning.* Mawah, NJ: LEA.

Stanovich, K.E. & West, R.F. (1997). Reasoning independently of prior belief and individual differences in actively open-minded thinking. *Journal of Educational Psychology,* 89, 342-357.

Stanovich, K.E. & West, R.E. (1998). Individual differences in rational thought. *Journal of Experimental Psychology: General*, 127, 161-188.

Stoddard, L. (1992). *Redesigning education: A guide for developing human greatness.* Tucson, AZ: Zephyr Press.

Tishman, S. & Andrade, A. (n.d.). Thinking dispositions: A review of current theories, practices, and issues. Retrieved 10/25/04 from http://learnweb.harvard.edu/alps/thinking/docs/Dispositions.html

Tishman, S., Jay, E. & Perkins, D. N. (1992). Teaching thinking dispositions: From transmission to enculturation. Retrieved 10/25/04 from http://learnweb.harvard.edu/alps/thinking/docs/article2.html

VanGundy, A.B. (1998). *How to create the ideal brainstorming session.* June 22.

Van Manen, M. (1991). *The tact of teaching: The meaning of pedagogical thoughtfulness.* Albany, NY: State University of New York Press.

Weissbourd, R. (2003, March). Moral teachers, moral students. *Educational Leadership*, 6-11.

Wilson, S., Floden, R., & Ferrini-Mundy, J. (2001). Teacher preparation research: Current knowledge, gaps, and recommendations. Center for the Study of Teaching and Policy: A University of Washington, Stanford University, University of Michigan, and University of Pennsylvania Consortium. Available: http://depts.washington.edu/ctpmail/PDFs/TeacherPrep-WFFM-02-2001.pdf

Zmuda, A., Kuklis, R., & Kline, E. (2004). *Transforming schools: Creating a culture of continuous improvement.* Alexandria, Virginia: Association for Supervision and Curriculum Development.

AUTHOR'S BIOGRAPHICAL SKETCH

The author is a 1976 Miami University of Ohio, Ph.D. graduate. He is currently a member of the Department of Educational Leadership and Policy Studies at Florida International University, Miami, Florida. His teaching responsibilities include undergraduate and graduate courses in social foundations of education.

His research interest is in the area of humanistic/holistic education and human science. His articles have appeared in *Florida Journal of Teacher Education, Teacher Education Quarterly, College Student Journal, Educational Foundations Journal, Journal of Humanistic Education,* and *Holistic Education (*now *Encounter: Education for Meaning and Social Justice.*

He has edited, *The Forum,* authored, *The Development of a Conceptual Framework: The Stimulation for Coherence and Continuous Improvement in Teacher Education,* co-authored, *Thinking about Education: Philosophical Issues and Perspectives, Teaching as Enhancing Human Effectiveness, Enhancing Effective Thinking and Problem Solving for Pre-Service Candidates and In-Service Professionals,* and *Bringing Out the Best in Human Effectiveness: Lessons for Educators from an Upward Bound Project.*

His book reviews have appeared in *Choice, Educational Studies Journal, Journal for Students Placed at Risk,* and the *Journal of Negro Education.*

He is a past president of the Southeast Philosophy of Education Society, the Florida Foundations of Education and Policy Studies Society, and the Council for Social Foundations of Education.

He has served as a member of NCATE's Board of Examiners, represented the Council of Social Foundations of Education on the NCATE Unit Accreditation Board, and has served as Chair of the NCATE Unit Accreditation Board's Standards Committee.